Blogging for Authors

by

Barb Drozdowich

Cover Design by Michelle Fairbanks/Fresh Design
Edited by Margery Walshaw

Library of Congress Control Number: 2016905621

TABLE OF CONTENTS

DEDICATION

I would like to thank the authors who took their time to help me make this book the best it could be. All my friends at Off the Page and Kay Vreeland as well as my wonderful editor Margery Walshaw - many thanks for your guidance.

Note of Thanks

I would like to thank you for buying one of my books!

I tend to focus on the technical tasks that authors and bloggers need to learn. As of this publishing I have 9 books in print and several more in various stages of completion. I'm always looking to be helpful - often creating books around subjects that I get a lot of questions on from authors and bloggers just like you.

At the end of this book is the link to get 2 FREE BOOKS filled with helpful hints and several videos delivered straight to your inbox. Also at the end of the book is a link to a WordPress for Beginners course (discounted price).

On to the book - I hope you enjoy and learn lots!

INTRODUCTION

WRITERS THE WORLD OVER are consumed by creating the perfect book. Characters, plot, setting, and dialogue all weigh heavily on the author's mind. Yet, in my experience, one significant factor isn't considered until far too late – the audience for the book. At publication, writers are often barraged by 'helpful' instructions – get a Twitter account – join Facebook – start a blog.

Finding that all-important reader is the key to a writer's success. To do so, one must learn to network and communicate. In this modern age of book publishing, blogging is crucial and by far the most important method of communicating with your readers.

Welcome to Blogging for Authors! My name is Barb Drozdowich and I'm a book blogger at Sugarbeat's Books and the author of nine books designed to help authors with technical issues found in the publishing world. I started book blogging in 2010 as a creative outlet and a mental escape from a house of kids. Book blogging allowed me to talk to other adults about one of my favorite subjects – romance novels – without actually leaving the house.

As my family got older, I found that my background in technical training gave me a variety of insights into blogging – a keener level of understanding that my peers didn't possess. My comfort with technical subjects quickly made me the go-to person for solving problems on my friends' blogs. Several courses later, and hundreds of hours of hands-on experience with building, posting to, and explaining how to use blogs, I found myself with a new full-time job. When I'm not writing, I create WordPress blogs for authors and teach blogging and other technical subjects to authors and other creatives. I have 20+ years of experience in teaching technical subjects in a collegiate and corporate environment. Now, I spend my days explaining technical issues in a non-technical fashion.

This book was born out of conversations with a lot of authors who struggle with the topic of blogging to communicate with their readers. Authors are creative – they can write an outstanding story, but when it comes to dealing with technical issues? Not so much. This book is aimed at the beginner to intermediate level blogger. If you have some experience, there may be some information in this book that you already know. You may find yourself skipping some sections, but I believe this book contains valuable information for all skill levels!

I certainly understand the challenges of launching your blogging career. I was there once and had to figure things out. That's one of the main reasons behind my creation of this book. My hope is that each chapter brings you closer to your blogging goals and the specialized Technical Help section and Glossary at the end of the book will help make sense of common problems that authors struggle with. Once you get to the end of this book, you can find a coupon code for 50% off an on-line WordPress course that I've created with authors in mind.

I'm here to tell you blogging can be fun. Let's get started.

Chapter 1 - What is Blogging

AT ITS HEART, blogging is just another form of communication. In my mind there isn't a lot of difference between blogging and having a chat with some friends over a cup of coffee. You'll notice that I'm using the words "chat" or "conversation." When we're talking about blogging, I want you to keep the word "dialogue" in mind.

A blog is neither a billboard, nor a monologue. Blogging should be a dialogue.

Although I refer to the words "conversation" and "dialogue," your first response may be that no one talks on your blog, or that no one leaves comments for you to respond to. Times have changed.

The face of a conversation has changed in the electronic world. The person with whom we are chatting may not literally respond with words – they might respond with actions such as sharing your post with their friends on Facebook. They are doing the electronic equivalent of "Come over here and listen to this person." The electronic version is more along the lines of "This is great information; please go and read it." That's a response and in the big picture, that's a much more important response. Although I'm the first one to admit that comments are wonderful, such interaction is between two people. I have 16,000+ followers on Twitter. If I share on Twitter, it's pretty likely that more people than just myself will be part of the conversation. It's also pretty likely that a handful of my 16,000+ followers will join in, in their own way.

If you have a WordPress blog, one of the people you are "speaking" to might click on the Like button or in fact be so moved by what you have to say that they re-blog it. And the conversation grows to include even more people.

The author's blog is a space that belongs to the author – unlike

Facebook, Twitter or other social media. The author's blog is also searched and indexed by Google unlike the various social media (for the most part). This allows for your conversations to be searched for and found long after they take place. This isn't true of any material that you put on most social media. In fact, a post on your blog can be found years after it's created. The accepted shelf life of a Facebook post is considered to be between two and five hours and the shelf life of a Twitter post is 18 minutes. A LinkedIn post can have a shelf life of up to 24 hours in some cases.

An author's blog is the place where the author can share with their community; the place they can start or continue conversations and have dialogues. This is the place that the dialogue will grow a community of friends and supporters – people with like interests who will help spread the word about your book.

The content shared is based on the author's personality and interests and should be reflective of their branding. Yup – there's that nasty word – branding. We'll talk about branding – how straightforward it is – and how it's often blown out of proportion. We'll flesh out the topic of what to blog about, but first of all, we'll talk about why.

CHAPTER 2 - WHY DO I NEED TO BLOG?

THE QUESTION that comes up repeatedly during my discussions with authors – Why? Why do I need to blog? There are several answers to this question. At the top of the heap, blogging is a writing exercise, another opportunity to develop that writing muscle. The second reason is to communicate with your readers and develop a community.

We all figured out how to make friends in Kindergarten: "Hi, my name is Barb. Do you want to play with me?" As adults in the electronic world, the way to make friends is admittedly a bit more complicated, but not impossible. It goes something along the lines of, "Hi, my name is Barb and I write books. Let's explore interests we have in common and chat about stuff over a cup of virtual coffee."

The third reason, as I mentioned in the previous section, is to communicate and share with your community of readers in a fairly permanent way. Unlike the other parts of your platform, your blog posts can be searched and found months or years after they were first shared. So a post that attracted a new reader into having a virtual chat with you two years ago could easily be found today and have the same effect on a new reader.

Your blog is your public face to the world. In today's society if we want to find out more about public figures, we "Google" them. Frankly, we expect all public figures including authors to have a website of some sort where we can find out more about them and their books. As we'll find out in the coming chapters, it's important to have a blog, but generally not necessary to have a website and a blog. A blog offers an author the ability to add fresh content on a regular basis to their site – something that Google LOVES!

Think of Google as a toddler. For those parents reading this, you realize that toddlers don't stay interested in anything for long. Even shiny, new toys are quickly abandoned for the box they came in. Google is similar. Google is attracted to new content. A blog that's posted to on a regular basis provides a steady stream of "shiny new toys" for the Google search engine. This helps a site rise up the ranks in a Google search. While it's true that the majority of your traffic will initially either come from your friends or be referral traffic from other social media, you want readers to be able to Google the genre they read and find your site in a search. We'll talk more about this in a future chapter.

One last comment for this section is about tone and language. As I've mentioned previously, I feel that your blog should be a conversation – a dialogue with your readers. A blog post that's a dialogue with your readers is typically casual in its language and tone, like a conversation between friends. It's meant to share information as you would over a cup of coffee or a glass of beer with your friends. If your blog post is more formal, it will sound like a dissertation or even a monologue. It may end up conveying information to an audience, but it typically won't turn your audience into a community. In short, your audience will react differently. Think about how you react when reading let's say a Wikipedia page. You're looking for information and you get it. Compare this to reading a chatty, personalized blog post. You'll have a different internal reaction.

I'll continue to remind you to keep the word "dialogue" in your mind as we go through this book. I find when you think of something as a dialogue, that is what you create.

Chapter 3 - What is Branding and What are Keywords?

BEFORE WE FIGURE OUT what to blog, I want to talk about two words that come up frequently, but are often not understood – Keywords and Branding.

Authors are told that their branding is SO important. But comments like this leave many authors scratching their heads in confusion. Let me explain.

Branding is the look, feel, and tone of your platform.

Branding encompasses everything from the colors you use in your book covers to the look of your blog and social media, to what you write about and what you say on various parts of your platform including your blog and social media sites. We can choose to see branding as very complicated and overwhelming, but I choose to see branding as very simple and straightforward.

Branding in terms of books can be illustrated with this example. Imagine you're in the middle of a bookstore, but there aren't any labels on the shelves referring to genre. Still, I bet you could wander the aisles and find the type of books you read.

Could you also scan the shelves and find the books of your favorite author? That illustration might be a bit tougher depending on whom your favorite author is and the genre(s) they write. Generally speaking, many books of a certain genre have a similar look and feel. If I look at the cover of two books – one a dark paranormal romance and the second a sweet romance – there should be a difference in the cover graphics. Typically, paranormal is much darker in colors and feel than a sweet romance cover. The covers of a mystery/thriller versus a cozy mystery are also quite different. I'm sure you follow where I'm going here.

When I look at all the books of my favorite author, they have a similar look. The colors are similar, the font is the same, the writing on the spine is identical (except for the different title words). They have a common branding as illustrated in a common look and feel!

If we use the same example of my favorite author and view her website, it has the same look and feel as her books. The colors are similar, the font used is the same as on her book covers. If I move further and look at her various social media accounts, I see the same graphic elements and fonts being used on all her accounts. I can tell at a glance if I'm in the right place.

Looking at the content of my favorite author's platform, I see a similar look and feel as well as tone to her content. One of the many reasons I like this author is because I enjoy what she shares. Perhaps I follow her accounts because we have common interests and I enjoy learning from her, or sharing what she has to say. I must admit that this author has been around for some time and is multi-published. She likely has had professional help with her branding and it shows.

Try this exercise: look at the platform of your favorite author – to make this fair, choose someone who is multi-published and has had time to work on their branding and see if you see what I'm talking about. For the ultimate test, look at a corporate brand like Nike or Starbucks or Coke. Corporate brands are often more defined – easier to see the commonality in look, feel, tone and content.

Like so many things we deal with as authors, branding is more of an art than a science. Branding touches on all parts of your platform to one extent or another. Since this book discusses blogging for authors, the aspect of branding that we'll focus on will be the look and feel of your blog to include colors, fonts, graphics, and content. The things that you talk about on your blog will go towards your branding – the tone, subject matter, consistency. You want readers to know what to expect from you – to have consistency. Once you conquer this part of the branding puzzle, you can move on and apply it to other parts of your platform.

Let's move onto the word "Keyword." When I Google "What is a Keyword?" Google tells me that a keyword is "a word or concept of great significance" or "a word to indicate the content of a document." This explanation makes the word "Keyword" sound important and I suppose it is.

In our everyday language the word "Keyword" is a bit overused. It seems to be used to refer to so many things. For the sake of this book we're going to look at Keywords in two different ways.

1. Keywords as they relate to how your blog ranks on a Google search; and,

2. Keywords as they relate to how you determine what to write on your blog.

We'll talk about Keywords as they relate to ranking in the chapters that deal with creating blog posts. However, the next chapter will discuss using Keywords to determine the content of your blog.

Chapter 4 - What to Blog about AKA Keywords?

ONE OF THE BIGGEST struggles authors have is: "WHAT DO I BLOG ABOUT?"

I can easily teach the mechanics of blogging – there are rules or at least guidelines to follow – but the content is more personal and can vary. Because of this, learning what to blog is often a "work in progress" type of thing. It's something you work at and modify over time as you get better and more comfortable.

Blogging is hard work and often authors make it even harder by not having a clear vision of what they want to say on their blog. As a result, they spend hours agonizing over every post – wasting good writing time. Unless an author has an idea of what they're going to talk about on their blog and have a plan in place, they often give up after a short time.

Remember, the main purpose behind blogging is not only to communicate with your readers, but to create and maintain a community of supporters of your books/work.

Let's see if we can attack the "What do I write" topic and help you figure out your path to creating content on your blog. What we're going to do specifically in this chapter is develop a list of words – you can call them Keywords – which you will use to guide the creation of content on your blog.

In the previous chapter we defined "Keyword." According to Google, "Keyword" is a word of great significance that indicates the content of a document. Moving from the more formal definition towards a more common description, it would be logical to say that an author's keywords are words that indicate subjects that are important and of interest to them; words that represent what they write about.

I typically describe Keywords by saying they are a small number of words that describe your books and the topics that interest you. What are you passionate about? I find that most authors are passionate about the subject matter of their books, or perhaps the time period their books are set in, but authors have other interests also.

You can certainly be passionate about breeding dogs as well as your historical romances set in Victorian England. Although we will be forming a list of Keywords to help determine what you'll blog about, you will use the same list for all your social media work.

To be clear here – I don't believe your blog should be a billboard of information about your book releases and sales events. I believe it should be a vehicle of conversation. Think of how you interact with your real-life friends. Think about conversations over a cup of coffee or a pint of beer with these friends. You likely talk about topics you have in common. You might talk about your work, but you likely talk about other topics as well. A blog is the same – you might mention your new book being released, but you'll also talk about other subjects that have nothing to do with your book, but are subjects that you're interested in and want to share with your friends – your community.

To help you determine what you're going to talk about on your blog, we're going to develop two lists of words or phrases – a simple one and a more expanded one that you will then use as a bit of a cheat sheet for blog topics.

Are you with me so far?

To help walk you through the process of developing your list of keywords, I'll use myself as an example.

I LOVE helping people understand technical subjects. I've spent decades doing this in various forms and with various subjects. So, that being said, what am I passionate about? If we use the starting point of helping people understand technical subjects, I then further define this with some Keywords:

- WordPress
- Blogging

- Social Media
- Self-Publishing or Publishing in general
- Book Blogging or bridging the gap between the book blogger world and the author world
- Canadianisms
- My lack of ability to function without coffee

You will notice when you look at the above list, not all my keywords have to do with teaching or technical subjects. I basically have major and minor keywords. The major ones have to do with tech subjects and the minor ones have to do with the non-tech subjects.

So…go get a piece of paper and write a short list of what you're passionate about. You may find that you're passionate about horses or about being an adoptive parent. There isn't a right or a wrong answer here.

Once you write down some things that you're passionate about, what are you instinctively drawn to or what do you seem to always write about/talk about. If you're already blogging, what do you prefer to write about? What words come easily to you? It's easier to talk about a subject that you're passionate about, than one you don't care much about or don't know a lot about.

Now that you have list of things you are passionate about, I want you to list some words or phrases that come out of that passion.

If I carry this exercise through for myself – using the shorter list above as a starting point, I can flesh it out into a more complete list by generating the following:

WordPress

1. Technical details of manipulating a WordPress blog

2. Some of the tricks of the trade to make WordPress easier

3. Designing WordPress blogs and how to take advantage of certain functionalities

Blogging

1. The "how-tos" of blogging

2. How to optimize various aspects of blogs

3. Current blogging news

Social Media

1. Social media management

2. Time management tricks

3. THE RULES and how to avoid getting in trouble on the various platforms

Self-Publishing or Publishing in general

1. How publishing has become a cottage industry

2. What is accurate information for authors, and what simply isn't true

3. Differences that make Canadian self-publishing unique

Book Blogging or bridging the gap between the book blogger world and the author world

1. Helping authors understand who book bloggers are and where to find them

2. Helping authors understand what book bloggers can do for the promotion of their books

Canadianisms

1. Canadian jokes

2. Canadian scenery

3. Things that are uniquely Canadian like Timmy's

My lack of ability to function without coffee

Needs no subheadings!

You see how I took a small number of central ideals or things that I'm passionate about and expanded it? I've essentially created a list of keywords with details.

Looking at the above list, how can you use it? I have mine posted on the wall beside my computer and use it as a topic helper. That way, it's handy when I sit down at my computer to put together posts for my blog.

As I'm sure you know, things that tie you to a recognizable group often automatically make you part of that group. Being Canadian makes me innately part of a group – either a group that my readers are part of or not. I frequently include Canadianisms, such as Timmy's, in my posts and generally get a response from many of my readers. The Canadians get the joke while others might ask what I'm talking about. Either way, it results in communication on my blog.

Here's an example: I created a post on following the rules of Facebook some months back. You'll note that the topic fits in with my list of Keywords. In the post I compared not following the rules on FB to not following common road rules. I said that once you get your driver's license, you get to choose which rules you follow and which you're more lenient with. I go on to question: How can you keep your hands at 10 and 2 and still hold your cup of Timmy's? (I even included a picture of a Timmy's cup of coffee.) Timmy's is an ultimate Canadianism, but very few people in other countries understand. This creates an inside joke for the Canadians, but I made it obvious enough for those reading the article who aren't Canadian. To date, this post has 19 comments and thousands of shares to every social media platform. By combining a tech post with humor I get a better response than by just lecturing. By using Canadianisms I can share the uniqueness of my country with my readers.

Every time I post a coffee joke on my blog, I get tons of shares and comments. Does my inability to function without coffee have anything to do with my books or my work? No, but it's funny at times, and it gives people an easy way to chat with me – to have a conversation. The same thing would work with puppies, kitties, kids doing cute things, beautiful scenery pictures, and the list goes on. I'm sure you've seen it happen on various social media platforms including blogs.

Let's go back to the first page of this book and why we blog. To recap: you blog to communicate with your readers, your developing community. You blog to have a dialogue. Every single person who comments or shares my coffee posts also shares in my dialogue.

The things you write about will help you communicate with your developing community. You don't need to write stories about adoption to write on your blog about being an adoptive parent. I don't need to write stories about characters drinking coffee to blog about an inability to function without it.

Are you getting closer to understanding what your Keywords are? While you're still mulling that over, let's talk about some blogging myths.

Myth #1: The only thing authors should post to their blog is information about their books - sales, releases, tours and the like.

This is obviously a myth as we've just spent several pages talking about how to use your blog to have a dialogue with your readers. I've actually heard "authority figures" preach that anything other than posting announcements/news on a blog is a waste of an author's time – it takes away from their writing time. Most authors I work with need to work at developing an audience. Posting announcements isn't going to start much of a conversation with readers.

Myth #2: Authors need to write about their book/their characters/their book's world on their blog.

That isn't to say that you can't mention your books – of course you can. But you want to use your blog to have a dialogue with a community of supporters, to help you promote you and your books. When you write blog posts about a book that's already been published (and a lot of people have read it) there's a frame of reference in your audience. This is different than writing blog posts about a book no one except you has seen. If no one has read the book, it's difficult for readers to relate. Yes, mention your book, but draw in your community using other things you are passionate about.

Myth #3: Authors need to write about their writing process.

Many readers are interested in an author as a person. This will include things like whether you have a puppy or a kitten living in your house, roughly where you live, other interests like hiking, traveling, etc. – points they can connect with. But the vast majority of readers won't give a rip about your thoughts on the Chicago Manual of Style. They may want to see pictures of your puppy, your writing desk or the view from your window as you create the wonderful stories they devour, but not grammar points.

Myth #4: Authors need to blog 4 to 6 times a week.

I find a heavy blogging schedule is difficult to maintain for long – especially for a beginner blogger. You simply run out of things to write about or you start resenting the time blogging takes away from all the other things you need to do. For authors just starting out, I suggest blogging no more than twice a week – one fun post and one more serious post.

Let's talk about what to blog about using the idea of creating two posts a week.

I think that these two posts allow you to be strategic with your time and yet maximize your networking opportunities. I like Wednesdays and either Saturdays or Sundays. When you choose those days, you can take advantage of two very popular memes (see below). Additionally, weekend readers typically have more free time to catch up on author news and therefore a longer, more involved post can be read.

Why Wednesday and the weekend and what are memes?

A Meme is a group activity – a group game that involves creating a post (in our case – on a blog and/or on a social media) and then following the rules of the particular meme, and visiting or interacting with other players of the game. The meme can be used to network with other players – to find friends or followers. Memes can be played on any social media, whether involving your blog or not. The two memes that we'll talk about are different from one another. One is a blog meme and the other is a Twitter meme.

The meme I often take part in on Wednesdays is called Wordless Wednesdays. It's a blog meme and it's possible to link your blog post to what's called a Linky so that other people can find it. (For more information on Linkys, see the glossary at the end of this book.)

On Mondays there's a Twitter meme I take advantage of called #MondayBlogs. This meme involves creating a post (on the weekend or any day you choose) and then on Monday post an attractive title and a link to the post as well as the hashtag MondayBlogs to your stream on Twitter. Then search Twitter for others playing the same meme and RT their posts liberally. Find posts of interest, people of interest and interact.

On Wednesdays I post a picture and a few words…that's Wordless Wednesday. Graphics of all sorts can be absorbed much faster than words – they're also language independent for the most part. AND it's easy. A picture of the mountain out of my office window or the sunset I captured on my iPhone can get a lot more attention than a post of words that I slaved over. As I mentioned above, if you want extra attention for your post – and find people to be friends with, join a Wordless Wednesday blog hop or Linky and spend some time using those connections to find people who share your interests.

The post on the weekend can be more involved with a combination of words and pictures as well as an invitation to join and "Friend." Although you might create and publish a post on the weekend, you can share it on Monday's Twitter meme: "#MondayBlogs." In a future chapter we'll talk about the strategies involved in creating a blog post and keeping attention on your blog.

Regardless of what you actually say on your blog, I have a couple of basic rules for blogging:

• If you're going to blog, it's part of your professional persona, therefore, you need to create a post that looks good. You can't fall back on the "I'm just not a tech person" excuse. To me, that excuse falls along the same lines as "I'm just not too good at grammar." There's a lot of help out there, both from myself and other qualified sources.

• As I've pointed out previously, blogging needs to be a conversation with your readers – a dialogue, not a monologue.

• Don't spend all your time apologizing.

• Don't spend a lot of your time being negative/critical.

In future chapters we'll learn quite a bit more information on blogging, but please keep the above four points in mind as you find your groove on your blog.

CHAPTER 5 - BLOG VS WEBSITE - PROS AND CONS - DO YOU NEED BOTH?

IN THE ONLINE WORLD there are two words that are used interchangeably – "Website" and "Blog." Do they mean the same thing?

Yes and No.

The word "website" historically refers to a static site on the Internet containing information that isn't changed frequently. Because new and exciting information doesn't typically appear in a timely fashion on static websites, these sites don't attract the attention of Google. We've already mentioned Google and its "shiny toy" mentality in a previous chapter.

Blogs by definition offer a constant stream of new information. Blogs, unlike what is traditionally known as a static website, offer a second benefit: the average person can maintain a blog with minimal paid help. Most important of all, a blog's fresh content ensures it will naturally rank higher in a Google search than a static website for the average person.

Today, "Website" and "Blog" are used interchangeably without distinct differences between them. In fact, an author site can be both website and blog. As you'll see in future chapters, it can contain information that rarely changes as well as information that is frequently changed. I recommend that authors not maintain two separate sites. Not only do they split their audience, but they double their work as well.

Years ago, a blog was known as a weblog, indicating that it was something found on the Internet as a serial recording of information—a diary, if you will. Today, blogs are quite different in terms of their appearance; they are personalized and modified to display information in a variety of ways. But ultimately, a blog is still a serial collection of information.

In my experience, many authors either start their blog on Blogger or on WordPress.com because they both offer a free platform. Whether you're still in the thinking stages of starting a blog or a seasoned blogger, I hope that by the end of our discussion of blogs you will have a better sense of the components required for a successful blogging experience.

This brings me to an important point—regardless of your web designer's opinion or your friends' opinions, ultimately your blog must be easy to use and tailored to your needs. If you have a blog that's too complicated for your skill level, ask for help. If you've paid someone to design a blog for you, ensure that the designer understands your skill level and creates something you are comfortable using.

Blogging is a very popular activity. In the year I started blogging (2010), Wikipedia tells me that there were about 152 million blogs already in existence around the world. I'm sure you can appreciate that the number of blogs has only increased since then. There are many different platforms for blogs. The most common include Blogger, free WordPress (also known as WordPress.com), and self-hosted WordPress (also known as WordPress.org). In addition, there is Tumblr, Squarespace, Weebly, WIX and a few others. Each platform has positive and negative aspects. For the purposes of this book, we'll be focusing on Blogger and WordPress as they are by far the most popular of the platforms. At the end of this chapter, we will mention the lesser popular platforms to round out our discussion.

Before we move on, let's define "blogging platform." A blogging platform is simply a program that runs the blog – just like an operating system runs your computer. In order for it to be seen by the whole internet, it is run on a mega computer at a company. We call this mega computer a server and we call the company the host or the hosting company. As you will find out shortly, there are a variety of programs that can be used to operate your blog and a variety of hosts that can run these programs. In some cases, the use of the blogging program and hosting is free and in other cases there's a monthly or yearly charge for that service.

"Can you run the blogging software from your own personal computer?" is a question I'm often asked. The short answer is yes, but it isn't something we do, for many reasons. The servers we use to run the blogging software are specialized for that purpose and designed to handle the traffic that visitors bring to a site. Your personal computer is not.

To operate a blog you'll need more than the platform and a hosting company. You'll need an address, which is also called a domain name (URL). When you guide someone to your blog on the Internet you supply the domain address, just as you provide a street address to visitors coming to your home.

On free platforms you can pay to register your own custom domain name, or choose to use their "free" or default domain name. Free domains typically include the platform ID. For example: http://firstnamelastname.wordpress.com

or http://firstnamelastname.blogspot.com. On paid platforms, such as WordPress.org, your only choice is a custom domain.

For authors purchasing a custom domain, your first choice – and my suggestion – should be your first and last name: http://firstname-lastname.com, if that combination is still available. If it's not, add the word "author" or "writer" before or after your name and see if that's available. For common surnames such as Smith or Jones, you might have to get quite creative to come up with a domain.

If you choose to have your blog on self-hosted WordPress, I also suggest that you purchase what's called "privacy" along with your domain. This keeps your personal information private and stops spam mail and email from arriving in your inbox or your mailbox with offers to "help" you. It also prevents people from easily finding out where you live if they research you online.

The last piece of the blog puzzle is the theme. The theme is the part of the blog that controls what the blog looks like. The colors, the font, the positioning of various pieces of information are all controlled by the theme. While more intricate themes will cost a flat rate, there are a variety of free themes as well. All platforms offer a selection of themes for you to choose from and many platforms allow designers to customize them. We will talk more about themes in a later chapter.

Just to be clear, a blog consists of four parts: the platform or program that runs it, the hosting or where it lives, the domain or the address, and the theme or the look of the site.

If you decide on self-hosted WordPress, make things simple and register your domain through the hosting company you choose. That way, you will pay one bill each year – combined domain and hosting. You won't have to keep track of different bills from different sources. If you decide to go with one of the other choices of platforms, you will most likely register your domain through that platform. There are other ways of doing this, but if you're just getting started and this whole process seems intimidating, keep it as simple as possible. There are many different hosting companies available. There are great companies, average companies and truly horrible companies. Many factors go into making a recommendation and I'll provide some basic guidelines in the next chapter. However, if you need help deciding, don't hesitate to contact me directly.

As I'm sure you'll determine as we move forward, my preference for blogging is self-hosted WordPress. As of this writing, operation of a self-hosted WordPress blog costs about $100.00 USD a year. There are some additional startup costs (for example, how much you spend depends on the graphics and theme selected for your blog). The costs both upfront as well as hidden are broken down in a future chapter.

If you decide to go with a "free" platform such as WordPress.com or Blogger, you can register a domain for a nominal charge. I'm not a huge fan of the long URLs that come with WordPress.com or Blogger blogs so I always suggest registering a custom domain.

Keep in mind as we go through this book and talk about various costs involved in operating a blog/website that regardless of what country you live in, the cost of a blog/website is a tax-deductible business expense. Keep your receipts and invoices and get some help declaring these expenses come tax time if you don't understand how.

Chapter 6 - The Blog Platform - Pros and Cons of the Choices

Blogger

LET'S TALK ABOUT the three popular platforms to host a blog, starting with Blogger. Blogger is free and hosted by Google. The only costs associated are the registration of a domain. As I suggested in the previous chapter, I feel that you should register a domain to avoid having http://yourdomain.blogspot.com as your domain. In my opinion, your domain should be your author name, not your author name combined with "blogspot." With Blogger, Google owns the program or platform and also supplies the hosting. It isn't possible to use Blogger's platform on an external hosting company. If you purchase a custom domain, you will arrange this through Blogger.

It is possible to hire someone to create a theme or a look for your site. It's also possible for you to work on the design elements yourself if you're looking for something simple and classic. This will save you the cost of hiring a designer as Blogger has a selection of preset themes that you can look through.

Posting to Blogger is straightforward. The posting window looks something like a word processing program. Adding various items on your sidebar is also quickly achieved. Simply choose from a number of preset gadgets and add them in the order you want. We'll talk about the details of this more in later chapters. In addition, there's a Technical Help section found at the back of this book that helps with various technical aspects of blogging. You can also access a large selection of YouTube videos I've made available to help with issues that may even trip up the experienced blogger.

Sounds good, right? It is, for many people. Complaints begin when users discover Blogger's limitations. Complaints range from:

1. You have only 1 GB to publish images. (Most people aren't aware of this until they run out of space and have to pay a nominal charge each month for additional space.)

2. You are limited to 20 pages. (Again, seems like a lot, but it's still a limit).

While I prefer WordPress and feel that it's more versatile, the average user finds Blogger works well for their blogging needs.

Rumors abound that Google shuts down some blogs running on Blogger for no apparent reason. This happens without warning, and all content is lost. Are blogs shut down for no reason? I don't think so. To remain in good standing you must adhere to Blogger's Terms of Use: (http://www.google.com/intl/en/policies/terms/). Regardless of the reason for blogs being shut down, this has created a large group of disgruntled and vocal former Blogger users. In addition, there have been several well-publicized service outages that frustrate people.

Yet, even with the negatives, many people love Blogger's simplicity and would never use a different blogging platform.

Free WordPress

Before we move our discussion of blogs to WordPress, I often have people ask me how they tell if they have the "free" version or the "self-hosted" version. The easiest way to tell is to log on to your WordPress site and find the menu bar that runs down the left side of your screen. If near the top, there is the word "Store" you have the "free" version.

Free WordPress, also known as WordPress.com, offers a simplified version of the self-hosted WordPress program. Again, there are positives and negatives to a free WordPress.com site. Like Blogger, the posting window resembles a word processing program with formatting abilities and a selection of preset widgets that appear on the sidebars. Unless you purchase a custom domain, you will have a longer

URL for your blog address. The normal WordPress.com URLs are: http://firstnamelastname.wordpress.com.

If you choose WordPress.com, the platform or program will be supplied by WordPress.com and they supply the hosting as well. Like Blogger, you don't have the choice to use an external hosting service. If you choose to register a custom domain, it is easiest to do so from WordPress.com – directly from the dashboard of your blog, in fact.

Like Blogger, WordPress.com features a selection of preset themes or looks. You can choose among these preset themes, many of which have a variety of color, font and layout choices available. Again, the main complaint I hear about WordPress.com blogs is that you're limited in functionality.

Once you are confident and ready to spread your wings with regards to your blogging, you will likely find yourself limited. You have very little choice for themes or looks for your blog unless you pay between $20.00 and $120.00 USD/year for a custom theme. You are prevented from engaging in any sort of e-commerce (unless you pay $299.00 USD/year for that privilege), and your blog may show ads that you have no control over (unless you pay $99.00 USD/year to prevent them from showing). This list indicates that WordPress.com isn't necessarily free. As an author, you are running a business. Do you really want to allow WordPress.com to put ads for other products on your site – encouraging your readers to buy something other than YOUR books?

Ultimately, you need to operate your blog under WordPress.com's rules, which some bloggers find onerous. However, if you don't follow the rules, WordPress.com will shut down your blog with little to no notice.

These issues may not matter to you. If you simply wish to publish posts and communicate with your readers, WordPress.com, like Blogger, may be fine.

> **Tech hint:** Wordpress.com typically enforces its rules swiftly. According to the Terms of Service (TOS) found here (https://en.wordpress.com/tos/) you have to maintain your blog according to what some consider to be strict rules. Although often considered to be more important to book

bloggers, Wordpress.com doesn't allow what it refers to as Book Blog Tour blogs. In other words, it wants blogs that have original content, not repetitive content that's common on blogs that host tours. To ensure that you're operating your blog according to the TOS, make sure you review the above link. To encourage you, the TOS documents are very readable - not full of legalese.

Self-Hosted WordPress

As I've mentioned, I prefer the versatility of a self-hosted or paid WordPress blog (WordPress.org). The posting window is almost the same as WordPress.com, once again resembling a word processing program.

You can use one of the preset themes or hire a designer to make a customized theme. The sky is the limit for your blog's look. You are limited only by your imagination and budget; custom graphics can be fairly expensive, but you may decide you want a distinctive look. If you decide to go with custom graphics, carry your custom look through your various social media platforms and also your book cover graphics as this helps with branding. I'm constantly impressed by the creativity of authors and graphic designers. WordPress (as well as the other platforms to a certain extent) can be made to look amazing! Back when I started with self-hosted WordPress (2010), customizing a blog required some coding knowledge. Today's themes typically come with a "click on your choice" type of customization allowing you to choose colors, fonts and layouts by simply clicking on choices rather than having to code them into place. So much more convenient for the beginner!

With WordPress.org sites, the platform or program is free and can be installed at any appropriate hosting. You have the freedom to choose your hosting company. Although you can register your domain from a number of sources, I suggest keeping things simple. As I mentioned previously, if you register your domain from the same company as your hosting, you will only have one bill to deal with – less confusing for beginners!

When you have a self-hosted WordPress blog, one aspect to consider is that you become your own technical support department. You are responsible for backing up your blog, updating your plugins and potentially searching YouTube when something goes wrong and you don't know how to fix it.

As we will discuss several times in this book, make smart choices on your blog. Many themes come with tech support included in the price. The same can be said for plugins as well as hosting. You don't have to be nickeled and dimed to run a blog.

Other Platforms

The other platforms that are often used by authors are Squarespace, Weebly, Tumblr, and WIX.

Squarespace powers around 1.8 million websites. Compared to WordPress, which powers over 60 million websites, they're small potatoes. Although you can try out Squarespace for free, it's a paid service with packages ranging at the time of this writing from $8.00 to $26.00 per month. You are currently limited to 32 preset themes with some color/font/layout choices available. With Squarespace, the program is owned by the company and you have to use Squarespace's hosting. That leaves you somewhat confined by their rules, however many authors are attracted to the 24/7 customer support. People find Squarespace relatively easy to use and, like Blogger users, would use nothing else.

Weebly is a free "drag-and-drop" website builder. It claims to host about 20 million sites and has its supporters. Although it's frequently used for websites and e-commerce stores, it isn't commonly the choice of authors. Like Squarespace, the blog platform is owned by Weebly and you have to use their hosting. At the time of this writing, the packages range from free to $25.00 per month and only the upper level packages have 24/7 phone support.

Tumblr is a very popular platform with claims of hosting 221 million websites as of February 2016. Tumblr is considered to be a social media and microblogging platform. One concern continually raised in the literature is Tumblr's re-blogging functionality. There have been many complaints of copyright infringement by users. I have a Tumblr account and enjoy surfing through posts and finding things to read. I have, however, been frequently confronted by pictures that are not appropriate for my family's viewing. It could be that I need to choose my friends more wisely. That and the complaints of copyright infringement keep my involvement with Tumblr to a minimum.

Lastly, **WIX** is said to host 59 million websites. As of the writing of this book, prices range from $4.08 to $24.90 per month, with the most basic plan displaying WIX ads on the websites. It's considered to be a drag-and-drop website builder. WIX provides the program and you must use WIX hosting. They have a variety of themes available, but once you've chosen a theme, you can't change it.

I've used the WIX platform several times and have had the occasion to help friends with their sites. I don't find the WIX editor particularly intuitive. In fact, I find it downright awkward to use. WIX was originally created for Flash websites, which we no longer favor as they aren't SEO-friendly and are often slow to load. For me, those two issues are a deal killer. Combine that with the difficult-to-use editor, and I suggest that you look to a different platform to host your blog.

To finish off this section, I want to leave you with a few personal thoughts on your choice of platform. I certainly am fond of self-hosted WordPress due to the extensive research I've done on the topic. I think that as authors you need to focus on your strengths – writing – and depend on the research that already exists rather than trying to re-invent the wheel yourself.

There's a saying: "Follow the money." If you look at the platform of the major players in the communication industry, you'll find that they use WordPress as their platform. The New Yorker, Variety, Play Station Blog, Best Buy, Xerox, Bata shoes, Fortune and Time, Inc. all use WordPress.

Blogger has had quite a few well-publicized service outages as has Tumblr. Because you have to use the hosting provided by all my examples except self-hosted WordPress, you can be held hostage by issues that are outside your control. Most recently, Google delisted all WIX accounts. I'm sure Google had their reasons, but as a result, everyone who had/has a site with WIX disappeared from all Google searches. (See: http://theamericangenius.com/social-media/google-to-no-longer-index-wix-sites-more-proof-you-should-own-your-own-site/) You need to focus your energies on your writing, not fighting issues beyond your control within your website.

Thoughts on Design

Typically, blogs follow a common layout. They have a header that runs the width at the top. That header may be a graphic or simply text spelling out the author's name in a decorative font. Underneath the header is usually a menu bar that contains clickable links to other parts of the site. The rest of the site is likely divided into two or three vertical columns with a final block of space at the bottom. The main portion of space is taken up by your blog posts running in a serial fashion down the length of the site. Most blogs have a space to one side or both sides of this area – sidebars – that can contain information like follow icons, Goodreads badges and the like. The space that's found at the bottom of the site is called the footer. It can also have information such as a repeat of the menu bar.

Once you decide on a platform, give some thought to the look or design of your blog. Since I list book blogs on The Book Blogger List (http://bookbloggerlist.com), I'm exposed to a large variety of blogs. I know for a fact that many book bloggers and authors are incredibly creative and this creativity shines in their blog design! As I've mentioned previously, the look and feel of your website should be part of your branding. Just like when you go to a bookstore and find your favorite author's books because they carry a similar look, I believe this look should be carried through to your blog design as well as all your social media platforms.

That being said, I feel you should be able to express your creativity with the look of your blog. For those who haven't created a blog yet, or are thinking about changing, I think it's important to point out some design issues.

It's generally advisable to avoid designing a black blog with white or grey or red writing. This color combination is difficult to read. Likewise, a glaring white blog with small black or dark grey text is also hard on the eyes.

Keep in mind these additional suggestions:

• Stay clear of elements that flash or blink.
• Avoid glaring colors like fuchsia, lime-green, or canary-yellow (certainly acceptable as accent colors, but not in large blocks).

- If you insist on having music play on your blog, make it optional. Some people use work time to read blogs and having music that automatically starts playing from your blog could get your readers reprimanded at their job.

While no one could accuse me personally of being trendy, I think it's important to keep the style of your site up to date. The overall look of blogs follow trends just like women's shoes. When I created my first blog, the trend was to create sites with a graphical header, blog posts and one sidebar – usually with a colored or patterned background. Today, most blogs are created without a graphic header – just text spelling out the blog name or author name and a short, to the point, landing page. The blog posts are only visible by choosing to visit the blog section of the site. The majority of blogs are lighter in color and use compartmentalization to organize information. Although you may not care if you're fashionable – I'm on the same page – your readers will know if your blog is of an older style and out of date.

A key point that must be made before we leave this chapter on design thoughts is with respect to mobile responsiveness. Because of Google's changes, it's more vital than ever that you have a mobile responsive site. I'm sure your eyes just crossed and you thought…what NOW?

There are two kinds of mobile responsive sites. One type is where the site properly scales (gets smaller or larger) to fit a variety of screens. The second reorganizes the content to a different orientation – typically a more vertical arrangement – with a menu that has to be clicked on to be expanded and used. For several years, the first description was what was required to qualify as a mobile site by Google. Last year, Google brought in new rules and many web designers were scrambling to meet the somewhat unexpected requirements. Google has threatened to affect the ranking of what it considers non-mobile sites, but we aren't seeing that occur yet.

How do you tell what your site is? The easiest way is to look at it on your phone or tablet. What happens? Does it scale or reorganize? According to Google's rules, ideally it should reorganize.

Here are two examples. At the time of the writing of this book, my business site (http://bakerviewconsulting.com/) is an example of the first type of mobile responsive. It can be viewed on big screens as well as phone screens as it scales properly, but on a phone it does become somewhat difficult to navigate. Changing this site is on a to-do list, but clearly there aren't enough hours in a day...

An example of the second type of mobile responsive is the one for my favorite coffee shop – Tim Horton's (http://timhortons.com/). If you look at this site on a desktop screen it's nicely laid out horizontally. If you view it on a phone, the blocks of information move to become vertically organized and the menu changes into a 3-bar icon in the upper right corner.

If you find that your site isn't mobile responsive, you might consider making some changes. It is possible to adapt an existing theme to make it mobile responsive, but often it's easier to just choose a theme that's already designed to be mobile responsive.

Chapter 7 - Costs and Hidden Costs of Operating an Author Blog

IN MY EXPERIENCE, many authors hesitate to start blogging because they're wary of the technology, but also because they fear the costs associated with a blog. Before we start this topic, please realize that the expenses are lower than most people suspect. Furthermore, all costs involved with an author website – from domain and hosting to theme creation to instruction on operation – are considered a business expense by the tax collectors of most countries. If you don't already have a writer-friendly accountant, many writers' associations can provide you with names of knowledgeable folk in your area.

Let's break down the obvious costs and talk about possible hidden costs. I'm going to discuss costs broken down by platform, starting with Blogger.

Blogger

On the surface Blogger is free. It provides a default domain (http://firstnamelastname.blogspot.com) and the hosting for no charge. The companies that you can purchase a custom domain through will depend on the country in which you live. For bloggers in Canada (where I live), we're currently allowed to use EasyDNS, Godaddy.com, ix web hosting, 1 and 1, Yahoo Small Business, and No-IP. Although these companies periodically offer sales, a domain will typically cost between $10.00 and $15.00 per year. To see your choices, log into your Blogger account, go to Settings and then Publishing. You can access a list of choices for the country you live in and instructions on how to go about registering a domain.

As I said previously, Blogger has a wide variety of themes available for use from its dashboard. There are a large number of companies that offer free blogger themes as well as themes for a nominal charge. It's also possible to hire a designer to create a custom theme for your site. Designers' fees will vary according to a lot of factors. Ask around and get a referral; ask up front about the charges.

The last possible fee is for additional space. Blogger comes with 1GB of space, which seems like a lot but like the hard drive of many personal computers, it can become filled up over time. If you exceed your space limit, you will be charged about $5.00 per year for additional storage.

WordPress.com (free WordPress)

Like Blogger, on the surface WordPress.com is free. When you set up an account, you get a platform based URL that looks like https://firstnamelastname.wordpress.com/ and the hosting is supplied. If you choose to have a custom URL or domain name, you can purchase one through the WordPress dashboard (or anywhere else you choose). If you purchase a domain through your WordPress.com dashboard, the costs will be in the range of $18.00 USD per year.

The biggest pet peeve I have with WordPress.com is that you have to pay a fee to prevent ads from appearing on your blog. To stop the ads you must purchase either the Premium service ($99.00 USD per year) or Business service ($299.00 USD per year). Since your author blog is your professional face to the world, it doesn't seem right to me to try and sell your books while competing with other ads that WordPress puts in place.

WordPress.com sites have access to a number of free themes and for an additional charge you can make changes to some of the themes (like changing colors and fonts). There are also premium themes available for purchase. At a quick glance, the prices range from a few dollars to as much as $175.00 USD. WordPress.com doesn't allow themes to be created for your site by an external developer, but there are seemingly several hundred free and paid within the system to choose from.

Like Blogger, with WordPress.com sites, you can run out of space. Also like Blogger, you can purchase more space. On WordPress.com you start with 3GB of storage (more than Blogger's 1GB) and if you need more space, you need to purchase what is called <u>WordPress.com</u> Premium for $99.00 USD per year. This not only gets you more space, but a custom domain and the ability to purchase a custom theme (and the previously mentioned removal of WordPress ads).

<u>WordPress.com</u> prevents users from a variety of functions. You can't acquire or purchase new plugins and you can't carry out e-commerce. The e-commerce ability can be purchased for $299.00 USD per year. You are actually purchasing what's called <u>WordPress.com</u> Business, a package of features, including the ability to carry out e-commerce.

Please keep in mind that e-commerce is not selling or promoting your books. E-commerce is an on-line store – not linking a few books to Amazon.

WordPress.org (self-hosted WordPress)

Self-hosted WordPress is the one platform that can give you the freedom to make a wide variety of changes to your theme. Kind of like building a house in which you get to make every choice, the same is true for this platform.

Self-hosted WordPress sites require a domain, hosting, and a theme. A domain can be purchased from quite a few vendors, and as such, pricing will vary depending on the vendor and whether or not they have a sale. Typically, the price is in the $10.00 to $15.00 per year range. As I mentioned in the previous chapter, I strongly suggest that you purchase Privacy for an additional $10 or so per year. What this does is mask your personal details like email address and home address from the curious. Although it's unlikely that a potential stalker will try to find you through your website, companies regularly acquire information like your email address and home address to solicit you to purchase their services. If Privacy is purchased, this nonsense is prevented.

Self-hosted WordPress sites need to be hosted somewhere. The price of hosting can vary widely from about $3.95 per month to about $8.00 per month, but can be as high as $30.00 per month for high-end, tightly-secured hosting. This bill is typically paid annually and many companies will offer a price reduction for purchasing multiple years.

They also may offer a free year of domain registration at time of purchase or a free year of e-mail.

There are a lot of different companies that offer hosting. Everyone has an opinion as to what makes a good company. I tend to look for a company that has 24/7 phone support and very little down time in their service. There are a lot of different features you won't care about when you're just starting out. The amount of space provided for a basic account is typically sufficient and the amount of traffic allowed for is more than generous. Once your site grows and attracts a large audience, you may have different needs than you do at the beginning. Looking at a variety of peer reviews, it seems that Site Ground, iPage and InMotion are currently the top three hosting companies based on the experts.

Feel free to do your search of Google and see what you come up with. In my experience, there are a lot of companies that will be just fine in hosting your site. Typically, once a WordPress site is set up, it just ticks along like a clock with very few issues if taken care of properly (we'll talk about its care in a future chapter) and rarely needs fancy add-ons that some hosting companies may try to up-sell.

Your WordPress site will also need a theme. As with WordPress. com sites, there's a selection of free themes available for budget-conscious bloggers. Although they might be a decent starting point for the beginner, I feel that free themes give you what you pay for. I'm personally a fan of Genesis-based, premium themes from StudioPress, Web-Savvy Marketing, or other designers. These themes cost money, but are stable, regularly updated and most importantly, have great instructions available to set them up as well as access to a help forum for questions that may come up.

The next step up from premium themes is to hire a designer to create a custom theme for you. The prices designers charge is based on their education and experience and can vary widely. If you choose to hire a designer, make sure the one you hire has experience creating sites for authors as we are a niche group with special needs. Also, make sure that the designer is aware of your skill level and creates a site that you are capable of using and maintaining.

In terms of other costs, the sky is the limit with WordPress.org sites (self-hosted). It's possible to purchase custom plugins that perform a variety of functions on your blog from creating forms that collect information to specialized share buttons. It's also possible to pay for backup services and security services. The vast majority of these costs aren't necessary for the budget conscious author. A basic site with quality hosting and a branded, stable theme will allow for ample communication with your readers. There are a lot of free services and plugins available for your site. Take advantage of them, but be smart when making your choices.

I hope this chapter helps you understand the costs involved in having a blog. But just like when buying a new car, say no to the bells and whistles in order to keep yourself on budget.

Chapter 8 - The Blog - What Should it Contain?

MOST PEOPLE know that your blog will contain blog posts, the aspect of owning a blog that most people slave over. But there's more to consider. All blogs contain posts, but they will also contain pages. Let's talk about the basic content of your blog.

At a minimum, your blog should contain:

- An About Me page
- Books page
- Events/Appearances/In the News page
- Media page
- Contact Me page
- Blog Posts
- Sidebar(s)

To begin, you need a selection of pages to present information about you and your books in an organized fashion. We'll run through a list of potential pages, but keep in mind that your blog is your blog. It should reflect your personality. Just because I say you need a page entitled "About Me" feel free to use whatever title you find appropriate. Let your personality shine through.

CHAPTER 9 - WHAT'S THE DIFFERENCE BETWEEN POST AND PAGES?

BEFORE WE GO any further, let's talk about posts versus pages. Pages are areas of your blog where information can be recorded and usually accessed from the menu bar or the sidebar of your blog. Posts are part of the serial records of your blog. They're designed to appear one after another in a journal fashion.

So, what's the difference, you ask? Pages are intended to be a more permanent part of your blog and the intent is that there are only a handful of them created (in fact several platforms limit the number of pages that can be created). Posts, however, are theoretically infinite in number and are formatted to appear chronologically on most blog platforms.

In terms of their functionality, they can both have text formatted in a similar fashion to any word processing program. Words can be changed to appear bold, italicized, a different font or size, centered, justified, etcetera. Both can have pictures or videos embedded. There's more information on this in future chapters as well as within the Technical Help section at the back of the book where you can find links to a series of YouTube videos that I've created.

Before we cover posts, we will describe the types of pages needed by the average author. As I stated above, I suggest that all author blogs have a minimum of five pages—an About Me page, a Books page, a Media page, an Events/Appearances/In the News page, and a Contact page. Lastly, if you're going to review books on your site, you should have a review policy for several reasons that we'll talk about. Let's start with the About Me page.

About Me Page

Compile information about yourself in an interesting and compelling fashion. Readers want to know about you; they want to find a point of connection. You might assume that people will read your blog only because they read your books and want to keep up to date. That isn't necessarily true. I read a lot of blogs because I like the writing style of the author or because I enjoy their commentary. I don't have to read their books to suggest them to friends.

In addition to a blurb about you, I also suggest that you include a photo of yourself or a photo that will represent you—a so-called Gravatar. This site is the professional representation of you. Many people feel that you need to have a professional headshot done to use on your site as well as in promotions. It's not uncommon for authors to choose to be represented by a graphic or an image that isn't of their face. Although I understand the desire to remain anonymous if you're writing a genre you don't want to share with your neighbors, keep in mind that it's difficult to be truly anonymous on the Internet.

Your About Me page doesn't need to be your bio. It can be more extensive that that. It can be your philosophy on writing and what led you to do what you do. It can also be a commentary on what you're hoping people will get out of your site. It's your chance to connect and share.

Books Page

All authors need a page called "Book(s)" or "My Books" containing a list of the books they've published. For each book listed, include a cover graphic, a blurb, a link to an excerpt (that either can be downloaded or can be read on your site), hopefully a link to a page of reviews and all the available buy-links. Each entry (book) should be neatly divided from the next. If any of your books have won awards, feel free to show the award graphic or copy.

If you've written several books in a series, provide information on reading order, and preferably a synopsis of the storyline. This can be a separate page or simply an addition to the Books page. If a reader unknowingly begins with one of the books in the middle of the series, adding this information to your Books page will give a context for the entire series. Also consider including an FAQ section to help readers with questions about the various characters or storylines.

If you create a series of books with interconnected characters, provide some sort of graphic to help readers connect to your books. A family tree graphic, as an example, may serve the purpose. Ensure any graphic used displays well on the blog, or can be clicked and viewed in a larger size. As a regular reader of series books, let me assure you, readers love background information!

The historical romance series I read often contain as many as 8 or 10 books. It may take the author 4 or 5 years to complete the series. By the time I read the last book, I need help remembering the characters of the first one. Like many bibliophiles, I often read several series at once. The author knows the characters and storylines, but I often have trouble remembering what happened in the first book once I've reached the eighth. Before picking up one of my favorite author's new releases, I often go to her website and refresh my memory. You can do the same on your "Books" page to help your readers.

Media Page

The next page you will want to create is a "Media" page. The purpose of this page is for bloggers and other media professionals to quickly access information about you and your books. Most people don't realize that book bloggers can be charged with copyright infringement in some countries for using long excerpts or other commonly used items as part of a posted review. Does this often happen? Of course not. But you want to be as helpful as possible in the promotion of your books. When building this page for clients, I start the page with copy along the lines of this:

"All information on this page can be freely used in the promotion of the author's works."

Your Media page should contain your author picture and several versions of your bio. I've heard people suggest that you should have short, medium and long bios. Personally, I think this is excessive, but you should have a two-or three-sentence bio as well as something a bit longer, say 6 or 8 sentences.

You can also include a high-resolution cover graphic of each book along with the blurb. Although this information is on your Book page, the Media page should contain a rougher setup that allows for ease of use by review sites. Links on this page are not embedded; they're written in full to allow easy copying and pasting by an interested blogger.

Each entry can have all the associated buy-links beside or directly below it. Remember to be as helpful as possible to the people interested in promoting your books.

Lastly, you will want to list all your social media contact points, not necessarily as embedded links, but in long form so they can be copied and pasted as well.

Events/Appearances/In the News Page

The next page that I suggest is either an "Events/Appearances" page or an "In the News" page (or both). An Events page lists your current or upcoming appearances. Maybe you are having a book signing at the local bookstore or coffee shop, or setting up a signing table at a book festival in the next city. Make it easy for your readers to find you at promotional venues.

An "In the News" page lists your recent interviews, book reviews with links and stops on your latest blog tour. You will build goodwill with a book blogger if you link to her site. Finding her blog linked to a favorite author's site can make a book blogger's day! It's a great way to make friends.

It's also important to publicize your successes. Do I suggest you link to every review? No, of course not. If you do, you may engage trolls.

A troll is someone who leaves negative comments, disrupting the reviewing process. The troll likes to get you and your readers upset. Responding to the troll encourages them. It doesn't matter if the troll is a reader or an author. Do not engage with them.

You're probably thinking, "Which reviews do I link to and which do I ignore?" Select your reviews by the site location and by reading each review. If you are reviewed by the NY Times, absolutely list it! Most of us receive our reviews from book bloggers and/or Amazon reviewers. If a review is particularly complimentary and balanced, post a link to the review on your page and thank the blogger/reviewer for the review. Should you comment on reviews found on Amazon or even Goodreads? No. These are potentially shark-infested waters! Amazon and Goodreads are public forums open to anyone wishing to comment. Simply thanking someone for reading your book demonstrates good manners; questioning the review's veracity will only lead to trouble.

Keep your Events page up-to-date. Readers don't care if you were interviewed five years ago. They crave recent information. However, if you are well-published, you may list older reviews. Periodically check the posted links to ensure the blog that reviewed your book is still live. If the blog has been taken down, delete the link from your Events page.

Contact Page

It may seem like a no-brainer to create a Contact page, but in the hustle to finish a site, often the easiest things are the ones that are overlooked. You should provide an obvious method to contact you. The most common method is a contact form. This will allow your email address to be hidden from readers trying to contact you. It also provides a form that guides what people send you. If you're reviewing books on your site and take submissions, this form can serve double duty as a submission form.

If you choose to offer an email address as a contact point, ensure that the email address is hot-linked (or a clickable link), allowing readers to just click on a link to open an email form. This prevents readers from being forced to copy and paste your email address (and potentially making errors).

I recommend not offering anything like a phone number or house address on your site. If you wish to offer a mailing address, consider getting a P.O. Box for personal safety.

Review policy (if you are going to review)

As I've commented before, some authors review books and some don't. This is a preference; there isn't a right or a wrong. If you decide to review books, I believe that you need a Review policy. On this page you can outline how your reviews are structured. If what you do is post your thoughts about books that you get from the library or NetGalley or Edelweiss, and you aren't open to submissions of any sort from authors, state that. If you review submitted books, state what genre(s) you prefer to read. Even if you think you will review all genres, be honest about what your favorites are. Also be honest about other details like length of book, heat level of romance, goriness of a horror novel, etc. For example, I refuse to read anything over 350 or so pages as I find longer books overwhelming. I don't read horror as it gives me nightmares. The sexual explicitness of a book doesn't offend me, but I don't want to read romances involving anything other than human beings. What are your specific thoughts? Make note of them on your Review Policy page.

You might want to include information about the content of your reviews. How do you format your thoughts? Do you include spoilers? Do you offer up any quotes that an author can then use in promotions? Do you rate a book using hearts, stars, hopping bunnies, or flashing numbers? Do you post negative reviews? Do you post your thoughts about books that you were unable to finish reading? Do you post copies of your reviews on Amazon, Barnes & Noble, Goodreads, Booklikes or other locations?

If you participate in book blog tours from promotion companies, you might want to include that information on your Review policy also. You may consider listing the companies you work with.

Lastly, you can include how you want to be contacted and what information you need to consider when featuring or reviewing a book. I know I prefer to be contacted via email, but you need to state your preferences so authors will have clear instructions to follow.

Are there more pages you may need on your blog? Certainly! If you accept advertising, many bloggers have a page that outlines their advertising policy. There are requirements by the Federal Trade Commission (FTC) in the U.S. that indicate what's required if you collect advertising money or post reviews of books. Even using Amazon affiliate links to keep track of sales from your site requires a FTC statement. More on that in Chapter 19.

This is the end of our section on Pages and we're going to be moving on to Posts, but remember, if you are on Blogger, you're limited to 10 pages whereas on WordPress you're only limited by your creativity.

Chapter 10 - Blog Posts and Parts and Pieces

NOW THAT WE'VE DISCUSSED some of the pages you should include on your blog, let's discuss the design of your blog post area. This is the portion of your site where you share information in a chronological diary of entries. For the sake of this book, we're going to divide a blog post structurally into A) header (the area at the top), B) the body (in the middle), and C) the footer (at the bottom).

A) Post Header

The post header is the information at the top of the post and includes the blog post title, often the date, the author's name, and a place where readers can leave comments.

1) Post Title

The most obvious section of the post header is the post title. The most important point about a title is that it should be compelling. If you're going to share it on Facebook or Twitter, it can contain one or two hashtags. A title of a blog post that is filled with hashtags is difficult to read. If the post is about another author/blogger, feel free to include their Twitter handle in the title. Because of Google's limitations be careful of the number of characters. The ideal title is limited to 70 characters. Any longer and it's truncated when it appears in a Google search result. For those of you wanting to spend a bit more time on creating the perfect title, there are some websites such as http://coschedule.com/headline-analyzer that will help you fine-tune your ideas.

2) Date

I don't feel that a date field is necessary for author blogs. The majority of posts on Author blogs aren't usually date sensitive, unlike Tech blog posts. For this reason, the date field can be removed on most platforms.

3) Author

The component of the blog header that we'll talk about next is the name of the person posting the article, or the "author." On WordPress, the author is generally the username of the person signed in to the blog when creating the post, although that can be manipulated.

People are used to seeing usernames that consist of a first initial and a last name. I feel it's better to use your full first name and surname as your username. (If you're trying to remain anonymous on your blog, ensure that your "pen name" is showing as the author or username.) This is something you will want to give some thought to. You don't have as much flexibility on Blogger as you do on WordPress, but with some forethought, creative usernames can be generated. On WordPress, you can change how readers see your Author Name by changing it on your User Profile page or on a post by post basis.

4) Comments

Comments are another hot topic. Whether the point at which a reader accesses the ability to leave comments on your blog is at the beginning of your post or at the end, it should be obvious, and leaving comments should be easy to do. Let's talk about both of these issues.

There are probably several hundred different ways to control the look of comments, from fancy plugins with CAPTCHA (Completely Automated Public Turing test to tell Computers and Humans Apart), to the ability to leave cute smiley faces with the comment. In reality, experts tell us that on average only a small percentage of people who read our blog posts actually leave comments. Shouldn't we make it as easy as possible for these brave souls?

Many blog owners feel that it's necessary to go to ridiculous lengths to avoid spam. Some simply don't know how to change the settings to prevent a reader from jumping through hoops to leave a comment. In doing so, they create an unfriendly environment for readers to share their thoughts.

Spam happens. It's fairly simple to ensure that spam is held in moderation or segregated into a spam folder. Most WordPress blogs can be enabled with Akismet (see the chapter on plugins) or another anti-spam plugin. Blogger has similar systems available, and once configured, these plugins do a decent job of dealing with spam without making readers hand over their firstborn simply to leave a comment.

Whether the prompt to leave a comment is at the top or the bottom of your post, make it visible. Use a brighter color if necessary, and don't make people search for the comment field. Once people find the right spot to click on, don't make them log in. And for heaven sakes, don't make the reader enter those CAPTCHA letters. I've been known to give up without even trying when I'm faced with those blessed letters, and I know I'm not alone in that!

However you decide to combat spam, ensure your method doesn't result in spam appearing to the readers visiting your blog. Not only is it unprofessional to let people read comments about Viagra on your blog, it's an indication that your blog isn't set up properly and is a reflection of your skill level. Ask for help if you don't know how to put spam protection in place.

I have more details in the Technical Help section at the end of this book. If you want help putting your spam protection in place, see this section.

B) Body of the Blog Post

Let's talk about the body of the blog post. Make sure the background color, font style, and font color are easy on the eyes. The blog post must be easy to read or viewers will leave early. When I design blogs, I usually increase the font size from the default (which is often 12 pixels) to 14 or 16 pixels, depending on the actual font being used. This makes the copy easier to read and the site more reader friendly. That being said, if you want a blog closer to what you might consider a work of art, you need to go with your vision.

Many studies have shown that people who read blogs (or any electronic sources) have the attention span of a gnat. They don't really read; they scan. They hop, skip, and jump their way through the first few paragraphs of a blog post that you have likely slaved over. Do you need to pander to this?

Well, yes.

There are strategies you can use to keep people's attention focused on your work. At the top of this list, you can create short paragraphs — no more than 4 or 5 sentences each. Divide up each paragraph with a subheading, or a short quote from the next paragraph, or a single line in a different size font. Allow people's eyes to take a break, and give them a reason to read further. Make sure you include graphics — if you are reviewing a book, grab a copy of the cover graphic from Goodreads (not Google). If you're searching for that perfect picture for your post, check out one of the free sites like Pixabay.com or Unsplash.com. They have a large selection of free photos that can be used to dress up your post. (For more suggestions of where to get pictures for your blog posts see the Technical Help section at the back of this book.)

The average blog post should be in the range of 700 to 1,000 words. It can be a bit shorter or longer, but it shouldn't be the equivalent of a university dissertation. Blog readers will lose interest and wander away.

A magazine format for blogs is very popular these days. This is the format that shows the first half-dozen lines followed by a "read more" prompt or button. I was recently reading a blog article about this format and they claimed that it makes a blog look more organized. I agree, yet while the magazine format belongs on many sites, give some thought on whether it's right for yours. I believe it encourages a reader to leave the post without clicking on the "read more" prompt.

Does that happen on your blog? Your analytics will tell you if people are leaving before reading much. Google Analytics will tell you the average time readers spend on your blog. If it's under a minute, you know your readers aren't reading much. (http://www.google.ca/analytics/)

If you're unclear how to put Google Analytics in place on your blog, see the Technical Help section at the end of this book where you will find a link to a YouTube video that walks you through the process.

Two skills that all people seem to struggle with in terms of blog posts are manipulating pictures or other graphics and embedding videos on their blogs. If you struggle with either of these actions, please see the tutorials at the end of this book in the Technical Help section. I've created a series of YouTube videos about these subjects. I have help for inserting pictures from a variety of sources, adding a link to the picture, manipulating the pictures once they're in place, and the use of my favorite plugin – Tiled Galleries – among other subjects.

Now that you've created a blog post, are you done? No! We need to think about the aspects of the blog post beyond just the content.

Linking In/Linking Out

There are several effective strategies for keeping readers on your blog. The first is to link (or hyperlink) to another post within your own blog. This gives readers something else of yours to read.

Let's say your blog post discusses your new book release. You can link back to the post where you revealed the cover for that release. Make sure you have the link open in a new window so the reader can easily navigate back to what they were reading in the first place. (If you are unclear as to how to put a hyperlink in place as a text link, please see the tutorial at the end of this book in the Technical Help section.)

In addition to manually linking to your posts as well as others' posts, it's possible to use a plugin to help with your linking. There are many plugins available to help with this. I often put "Editorial Assistant by Zemanta" in place on the blogs of people just starting out. This plugin has many functions, one of which allows you to link to related posts by other bloggers. Jetpack has a similar functionality and so does LinkWithin. If you are blogging on Blogger, you can embed free code at the end of your posts or in an HTML/Javascript gadget to perform the same functionality.

Not only is it friendly to link to other people's blogs, it's considered good for SEO, especially when the people you link to link back to you. The rules for Google algorithms seem to change daily; there's no guarantee that what puts you at the top of the rank today will help you tomorrow. However, practicing goodwill with other bloggers and authors can only benefit your blog.

Regardless of the official reason, it's simply nice to link to other people's blogs. It's a good way to make friends. I think it's pretty cool to be notified that another blogger has linked to my post. Do you know how to determine that's happened? On many blogs it appears in your comments as a "Trackback" or a "Pingback." Often it's first seen as a comment requiring moderation. Trackbacks and pingbacks can also appear in a special section of the edit post view.

Let's say you now have a compelling blog post of a good length. It's well-formatted, spell-checked, and linked to other posts published by you and at least one post created by someone else. Are you finished? No!

C) Footer

1) Signature/Sign-off area

I think it's important to "sign" your blog post. These "signatures" can range from a formal-looking plugin complete with your bio and your social media links, to a quick "'Til Next Time" and your name. In my perfect world, a signature serves as a call to action.

There are many reasons for adding a signature/sign-off. Putting some sort of a signature in place gives your posts an identifiable end. For those of us experienced in the blogging world, our eyes are accustomed to the format of blogs. We understand how to identify the beginning and end of a post without really thinking about it. But not everyone has the same level of experience. There are people out there who have trouble finding the end of one post and the beginning of the next one. Help them out by creating an official end for your posts.

Secondly, the signature can give your readers directions – instructions that you want them to follow. As I mentioned above, the sign-off can be self-serving as well as decorative. It can be used to remind readers to follow you on your various social media accounts or subscribe to your newsletter. I find it amazing that a high percentage of readers follow the instructions in my signature! Try it on your site and see what happens!

In the Technical Help section at the end of the book, I have a link to a video on creating signatures for your blog posts.

2) Sharing Buttons

We've already talked about making it easy for readers to comment on your blog. You should also make it easy for them to share your posts. It's my opinion (and well-documented in the literature) that share buttons are hugely important and not given enough attention by many blog owners.

Yes, it's lovely to get comments. But it's more important to you, the blog owner, that readers feel compelled to share your posts across their social media platforms. This heightens your visibility, and can quickly lead to more readers and followers.

Share buttons can exist in one of three places: at the top of a post under the title, at the bottom of the post, or they can float along the side. On WordPress, these buttons can be installed with a plugin. There are a large number of plugins that perform this functionality.

Blogger comes with preset share buttons at the bottom of each post. I'm not a fan as I feel they aren't obvious enough. I don't think readers should have to hunt for share buttons. Several of the plugins available for WordPress offer up code that can also be used on Blogger to perform the same functionality. A quick Google search should give you some suggestions.

I would suggest that you put share buttons wherever they are most visible – either at the top of your post, the bottom, or both. Many people are like me, bashful about leaving a comment. I read a lot of blogs and find myself nodding and smiling as I read along, but when I go to leave a comment, the only thing I can think of typing is, "Thanks for sharing." Frankly, I would much rather share the post with my friends. I have thousands of followers on Twitter. Isn't it more important that I share with my friends than I find something scintillating to say as a comment? One last point, if you have share buttons that float along the side of your blog posts, make sure that they don't cover the text of your post.

Tech Hint: Which share buttons should you include? All of them — Facebook, Twitter, StumbleUpon, LinkedIn, Pinterest, Google+, email, Digg, Buffer, Tumblr, and Reddit. I don't care if you don't have a Digg account. It isn't your job to determine how your readers share your information. It's your job to provide interesting content and encourage sharing. It's their job to share in whatever fashion they are comfortable doing.

In my experience, if a post is going to go viral, it happens through StumbleUpon. Include a StumbleUpon share button along with your share buttons, get your self a free account and click that button on all of your posts as well as your friends' posts and see what happens.

If you're still reluctant to include share buttons, consider that Google finds it very important how many times your posts are shared. To Google, sharing is an indication of quality content and influences search ranking. You want to rank on Google, don't you?

Chapter 11 - The Ideal Structure of a Blog Post

NOW THAT WE'VE TALKED about creating a strategy of what to write and the parts and pieces of a blog post, let's talk about the structure of the ideal post. As I've said before, readers have a short attention span when it comes to reading electronic sources. Fortunately, there's actual science behind the basic structure of an ideal blog post, which provide clues to engaging with your readers. For a visual description of what we're going to talk about in this chapter, see the infographic on my blog (http://bakerviewconsulting.com/2016/01/anatomy-perfect-blog-post/)

A Picture is Worth a Thousand Words

We always include pictures in our blog posts. The pictures we use in our posts can communicate a feeling. They can set the tone for a blog post, or explain a complicated subject in a graphic form – especially when we're talking about infographics – one of my favorite types of graphics.

Every post needs at least one picture/graphic, and preferably more than one. There are links to places to get pictures at the end of this book in the Technical Help section. You need permission to use every picture you put on your blog. The Internet is a big place, but bloggers are still charged with copyright infringement if they don't have permission to use a picture. Purchasing pictures from stock photo sites isn't expensive – merely a few dollars each. Photos grabbed from a Google search could cost you thousands in legal fees or worse, could result in malware on your computer.

That's right, we see the surface of pictures, but we don't see any code that may be attached to a picture or graphic unless we specifically know how to look for it. This code can be used to track a picture, allowing the owner to see where it's used, and it can also be used to do harm to your blog. The only picture that I don't hesitate to use is a cover graphic. However, even having said that, I generally don't grab them from a random site, but rather from the author's own website or Goodreads. According to the copyright laws in most countries, we don't have to ask permission to use a book's cover art in our blog post.

Creating Ideal Content

The content of an ideal blog post should be set up as follows:

- Title (H1)
- Introduction
- SubHeader (H2)
- Picture/Graphic
- Text Content
- SubHeader (H2 or 3)
- Picture
- Text Content
- Signature/Call to Action

Obviously this structure can be tweaked a bit, but the above should be viewed as an exemplary guide.

Let's start with the title. A title should be compelling. It's often the first thing readers see and should encourage them to read further. One thought to keep in mind as you create a post is the keyword(s) you will focus on in your post. Don't hesitate to use the cheat sheet of keywords you created and posted beside your computer! The keyword should appear in the title as well as several times in the body of the post.

All blog posts titles are automatically assigned an H1 tag – also known as a Heading 1 tag. This is something the coding within your blog does automatically. To Google and other search engines, an H1 tag indicates the main title of an article. Google also expects to see only one H1 tagged section in each post. Those of you who fuss with the formatting of the text in your blog posts, you probably already realize that you can highlight text and apply preset formats to it. Only use the H1 format once per post.

> **Tech Note:** As I said above, Google only wants to see one H1 tag per post. Since H1 indicates 'Post Title' to Google, by duplicating it in one post, you confuse Google. It will see multiple 'Post Title' and it won't be able to figure out which one is correct. For more information on using H or Heading tags when formatting a post, see the formatting text video listed in the Technical Help section at the end of this book.

The next section of your blog post should be an introduction. Give your readers an idea of the topic, and why should they continue to read. This introduction should be friendly in tone and not any longer than 4 or 5 sentences as we've discussed in a previous chapter.

The next section is a Sub-header. A sub-header line should be formatted or 'tagged' with an H2 tag. This tells Google that it is in fact a subheading, not another title. This sub-header can literally be a sub-header or it can be a quote from the coming paragraph that encourages readers to read on. It can be a question you then go on to answer. Many experts say that the picture should come before the first Subheader, but I'll leave that decision to you.

Follow this with a picture or graphic. Use the picture to set the tone of the post – to entertain – and mainly to allow your reader's eyes to take a short break from the text.

The picture (or Sub-header) is then followed by the first section of content for the post. Each paragraph should be short – 3 or 4 sentences. A slice of whitespace should appear between each paragraph, unlike in books where the paragraphs appear one right after another.

Use a variety of font formatting to emphasize words or phrases – italics, bold, and capitals all have their place in blog posts. A variety of colors for your text don't. Most people find it comfortable to read black or dark grey text on a relatively light background. They find it visually difficult to focus on text that's a series of different colors.

Once the first section of your text is finished, follow that with either a sub-header or a picture, followed by a second section of text.

The length of your blog posts should be suited to your audience. Posting long dissertations are generally frowned on as most blogs don't have readers who stick around to read that much but let your stats guide you. (More on stats will appear in a future chapter.) I would suggest that if you're just starting out blogging that you aim for 700 to 1000 words initially and then move on from there.

The last part of your blog post is what I refer to as a signature – some refer to it as a call to action. Both labels work. This last section should thank readers for visiting/reading your thoughts, share with them current news, and then give them some tasks to carry out. For instance, remind your readers that your book will be on sale, or that you will be signing books at the local library. Invite them to pick up a bargain or visit you at the signing. Other tasks they might carry out include:

- following you on social media
- signups to your newsletter
- subscribing to your blog
- sharing your post with their friends on social media
- even a reminder to post a review if they've read your book

Don't overwhelm your readers with tasks, but do give them suggestions. I always find it amazing how compliant readers are when you give them tasks to do.

Let's talk about two more tasks that need to be part of your blog post – linking and SEO. These can be very simple, yet in my experience, few people take the time to do it.

In a previous chapter I mentioned linking in and linking out as a way to keep people reading your material and remaining on your site longer. If I'm writing a post about the steps involved in backing up a WordPress blog, I want to make sure to include several links. First and foremost, I want to include some links to other posts I've written on this subject. This will allow my readers to create a robust picture of the subject.

I'll also want to link to one or two articles I used for research so that my readers can see that I didn't just make this stuff up – that I have references for my post. Often the blogs I link to are 'friends' of mine – blogs I read on a regular basis. Frankly, I link to other blogs for my readers to have other references, but also to encourage my 'friends' to link back to me. It's good for SEO and ranking on Google to have what are called "quality backlinks." These aren't the type of links that you pay someone on Fiverr to generate for you. These are organic links – a showing of support from your friends. A vote of confidence, if you will.

What's that expression? To have a friend, you need to be a friend. Be a friend in the blog sense of the word by linking to your friends!

Lastly, I want you to be aware of how your post will look when it appears on a Google search. If you aren't aware of what I'm talking about – Google search something. Look at each individual entry that comes up as a result. Each entry has a title (likely the title of the blog post), a direct URL to the post, oftentimes a date, and then the first 156 characters of the post.

I'm of the thought that when you create a blog post, you should let your creative side free. You should write what you choose. You shouldn't pick and choose every word carefully for maximum SEO benefit. You don't blog for Nike or Coca-Cola; you're trying to create a community of readers/supporters and you should be "you" on your blog post.

At the same time, it's possible to be "you" on your blog post, yet manipulate how your post shows on a Google search. To do this, I use a plugin called Yoast SEO – but there are a number of similar plugins. This plugin allows me to change the title that Google shows, and choose a focus keyword that describes the post as well as create a custom Meta description, which will replace the first 150-odd characters of your post and become a Google snippet.

Try out a few of the choices in plugins and see which one you like. We'll talk about this functionality more when we discuss Plugins and Widgets in a future chapter.

CHAPTER 12 - TAGS AND CATEGORIES

ONCE YOU HAVE a blog post you're happy with, you need to assign tags and categories to it. Think of categories as the table of contents of a book and tags as the index of a book. You will have a relatively small number of categories, but probably a much larger number of tags.

Let's talk about categories first. There's a technique amongst the pros called Siloing or Funneling. Proponents of this technique use categories to organize their posts into an ever-increasing complexity of categories. To further visualize this, think of a multigenerational family tree. The idea is that Google likes following logical pathways to get at your information. You can use categories and sub-categories, and even sub-sub-categories to create these pathways.

I find that most people write about a relatively small selection of topics, which can easily be organized into 3 or 4 primary categories. Each category can have several subcategories. Let's use my site as an example. One of my main categories is "Social Media." This can be broken down into subcategories of "Facebook," "Twitter," "Instagram," "Pinterest," and so on. I have another main category of "Tutorials," which is broken down into "WordPress.org," "WordPress.com," and "Blogger." Are you starting to get the picture? Experiment with your site and see what you come up with.

To move on to tags, remember my example of a book index. If you think about the index of a non-fiction book, it has lots of entries of which each one can refer to more than one page – or in our case, posts. When you choose tags for your post, try to think about words or small phrases that people will use to search for (and find) your post on Google. Each post can have between 8 and 12 tags – less if the post is short, more if the post is longer. As I'm sure you'll realize you will start using the same tags over and over again.

For those of you using Blogger, you're only allowed to choose what is called labels. Think of labels as you would tags.

Regardless of which platform you use, please ensure that you choose categories and tags/labels that can help your readers find content they are interested in as well as help Google search your site efficiently.

Chapter 13 - Plugins & Widgets

LET'S TAKE a few minutes and talk about the difference between plugins and widgets (or as Blogger calls them, gadgets). It's important to note that WordPress.com blogs contain only 'widgets.' WordPress.org blogs have both plugins and widgets. Finally, Blogger blogs have 'gadgets.' To make the following discussion a bit smoother, if you operate a Blogger blog, wherever I mention widgets, think gadgets. And, if you have a WordPress.com blog, ignore the discussion about Plugins as you don't have access to them. Sounds good?

Plugins are little bits of code that can be downloaded to your blog to perform a specific function. Examples of plugins are Akismet, which is used to deal with spam, or Yoast SEO, which helps augment the SEO (search engine optimization) of your site. Widgets are plugins that are used for a function on your sidebar(s). An example of a widget is a Text Widget, which holds code or other text to be displayed on your sidebar.

WordPress.com and Blogger blogs have more limitations than WordPress.org blogs in this area as the first two come with a preselected set of widgets and no flexibility to add more plugins.

Tech Note: I do realize that it's possible to manually insert code to add functionality to Blogger blogs and I provide some tutorials in the Technical Help Section at the back of the book, but this isn't as ideal or easy as working with WordPress.org blogs.

Personally, I prefer the flexibility that WordPress.org provides in terms of its plugins. I often find myself coming to a screeching halt and trying to figure out a work-around for certain things on a Word-Press.com or a Blogger blog that I simply use a custom plugin for on a WordPress.org blog. I guess you would say that I'm spoiled.

Although WordPress.org blogs come with greater flexibility, they also demand a bit more upkeep. The WordPress.org blog requires updating and other maintenance activities. Plugins should be updated shortly after the developer submits a new version. If plugins aren't kept up to date, they become a security hazard. Hackers have been known to gain entrance to blogs by taking advantage of security 'holes' in out-of-date plugins. That being said, plugins don't always play nicely together in the proverbial sandbox. If your ability to leave comments disappears or your sidebars change position or size suddenly after updating a plugin, generally the problem is a non-compatible plugin (or plugin update). Because of this, I suggest taking a look at the "public" side of your blog after every plugin update to make sure that things don't look funny.

Let's take a few moments to discuss the type of functionality you should add to your blog through the use of plugins and widgets.

1) Akismet

Spam happens. But consider this...if spammers can't find your site, what hope does the average reader? The job of an anti-spam plugin is to identify potential spam comments, and either put them in the spam folder, or hold them for your moderation. I've mentioned Akismet before when we were covering the subject of comments. This is a plugin that's commonly used to combat spam on your site. There are other plugins that perform a similar function. Choose one you are comfortable with.

Many anti-spam plugins will learn from what you identify to be spam, so make sure you mark spam comments exactly as that... "spam" – and not as trash. The important thing is to make sure your readers don't see spam appearing as live comments. Not only does that indicate that your site isn't set up properly, but it's not very professional to have readers exposed to spam comments about Viagra or quality sunglasses, or whatever the topic of the day is for spammers.

2) Social Media Follow Icons

One of the main things you want your readers to be able to do is to find and follow/friend you on various social media. This networking is one of the primary reasons for having a blog. In terms of plugins that support this, there are many. It's also possible to create HTML coding to put icons into place. (See the Technical Help section for further details).

I frequently use Social Media Feather or Simple Social Icons to put follow icons in place. Although most of the common social media icons can be found in either of these two suggestions, neither provides the icons for Goodreads or Amazon – two places I suggest you send your readers so they can friend/follow you. For Goodreads, I suggest one of their author widgets, which I find are great for attracting attention to your books.

For those of you using WordPress.com or Blogger, it's possible to use a widget to put individual social media contact points in place. I feel you can make better use of your site's sidebar real estate than to line up individual widgets. The only other option when using WordPress.com or Blogger is to code in HTML. Again, don't hesitate to have a look at my Tech videos to walk you through this task. There's a video that I call "The cheater's method of creating HTML using your blog."

3) Sharing Icons

Sharing icons are also an essential plugin for an author's blog. I frequently use the sharing aspect of the Jetpack plugin for this functionality. Lately, I've been looking in different directions for sharing plugins as I find the presence of a StumbleUpon plugin very important. As I mentioned in a previous chapter, it's my experience that if a blog post is to go viral, it will do so because it's been shared on StumbleUpon.

For those of you using WordPress.com or Blogger, sharing buttons are part of the platform. I'm not a huge fan of the sharing buttons on Blogger, but it is possible to add custom code if you want something different than the default.

4) Mailchimp Sign-up

As an author it's important to spend as much time as possible communicating and networking in locations you own. Other than your blog, your newsletter is an example of a location you own. There are many different platforms for sending out a newsletter, but my favorite is Mailchimp. Mailchimp integrates nicely into WordPress and is free till you have 2000 subscribers. To create a sign-up widget on your sidebar there are a number of plugins that will allow you to seamlessly connect your newsletter service (i.e.: Mailchimp) to your blog.

For those of you using WordPress.com or Blogger, you will put code in place to create a signup widget. If you decide to use Mailchimp, the code is supplied by Mailchimp and easy to add into a text widget (or gadget) and place on your sidebar.

5) Blog Subscription

There are several ways to set up a subscription to your blog. The most common methods use either a Feedburner plugin or the subscription portion of the Jetpack plugin. I'm fond of using Mailchimp for newsletters and blog subscriptions, but Jetpack and Feedburner work just fine.

For those of you using WordPress.com, the Jetpack subscription option is open to you and on Blogger, you can connect through a variety of different services including Feedburner and BlogLovin'.

6) Image Widgets

I commonly add pictures or other graphics to the sidebar of my blog. My favorite plugin for this activity is called Image Widget. This easily allows you to put pictures on your sidebar, hotlinked (linked to another website such as Amazon if the image is the cover of your book), and accompanied with a caption or a title.

7) Wordfence – or something similar

In today's blogging world, we sadly need help keeping tabs on the security of our sites. I'm fond of Wordfence, but there are several choices available. Wordfence is free and you can set it up to email you automatically when something suspicious occurs on your blog. It can also be set to lock out potential hackers.

Although WordPress.com and Blogger blogs can be hacked, you aren't allowed to add any extra security to your sites. Please make sure that your passwords are strong – and by strong I mean between 8 and 12 characters – made up of a collection of capital and small letters, numbers and symbols. Make it ugly! Make it unlikely to guess…don't use your cat's name!

8) Yoast SEO – or Similar

There are several plugins that can be used to augment the SEO of your site. As authors, I don't expect you to be technical experts, but you need to use every crutch you can. Several of the SEO plugins (my favorite is Yoast SEO) come pre-configured and don't require anything other than to put it in place for it to have a significant effect on your site. The SEO plugins also allow you to add extra description to your posts, pages, and for that matter, your entire site, which will help search engines determine your site's content. Many of them, Yoast included, allow for the formation of Twitter cards – the addition of a graphic to your tweets from your posts. Finally, these plugins help connect your blog to important sites that facilitate searching by Google, Bing, and the like.

For those of you using WordPress.com and Blogger, you don't have access to this help.

9) Updraft – or Something Similar

For the security of your blog, it is vital that you perform regular backups. I've found it extremely helpful to have a plugin that will back-up my blog on a schedule without any input from me. I, for one, am thankful that my blogs are backed up regularly, whether I remember to check or not. I'm fond of Updraft for this functionality, but there are quite a few choices. In fact, many hosting companies will offer to regularly back up your blog. We will talk more about creating backups for your blog in a later chapter.

Chapter 14 - Blog Sidebars

LET'S MOVE ON to sidebars. Sidebars are the areas to one side (or both sides) of your posting area. This is where you provide information that connects you to your readers in a variety of ways. As I like to point out, sidebars aren't like a closet in your hall where you stuff everything that doesn't fit anywhere else when company is coming. Sidebars should only contain necessary widgets and information. These widgets and information should appear from top to bottom in order of decreasing importance.

An author blog is a representation of you – of your business. As such, you need to be more formal than hobby bloggers and be careful of the use of your sidebar real estate. It is often said that you only have a few precious seconds to grab a visitor's interest.

I feel the most important widget to have on your sidebar is one that allows your readers to follow your blog posts on their social media. Although it's possible to get individual icons for every social media platform and arrange them down the sidebar, doing so takes up vertical room. I suggest putting one widget in place that includes all the icons in one spot. Although, as I mentioned in the previous chapter, there are a variety of plugins that can do this job on a WordPress.org blog, I encourage authors to point readers towards your presence on Goodreads as well as Amazon. The number of styles of icons available seems unlimited. Look around for a style that suits your branding.

Tech Hint: If you have a Blogger blog, a pre-set widget or gadget doesn't exist. It is often dependent on the blogger to create code to put the follow icons into place. Do you code? I don't really code, I cheat. If you want to learn how to do this the easy way, look for the tutorial on this subject at the end of this book.

Below the "follow" widget, I suggest a widget that allows readers to have your posts delivered in email form. This is referred to as Subscription and was mentioned in the previous chapter also. As authors we want people to subscribe to our blogs as well as our newsletters. The most accurate way to get readers to read what you write on your site is to have it sent to their inbox. As I write that, I have to admit that I rarely subscribe by email to blogs. I use a service called Feedly that allows me to subscribe to blogs using their RSS feed and I read all my blogs on one website. Periodically, I read a post that tells me that RSS is dead and you don't need to have it on your blog. I disagree. There are a lot of people, like me, who prefer not to have posts in my inbox, and use a feed service like Feedly. Make sure the RSS is present!

As authors it's important that we allow our readers to follow our site in whatever fashion works for them, and not limit them to the methods we choose. If that method is social media, so be it. We just need to encourage it.

And, since we're encouraging our readers to subscribe to our blog and newsletter, we need to be clear about what people are signing up for. Find a way to differentiate the choices to your readers so they understand what they are signing up for.

Inside WordPress.org, you'll find Jetpack. This collection of plugins offers a variety of functionality, including email subscription. This email plugin is perhaps the easiest method of arranging for email subscription on WordPress.org sites. It's also possible to use Feedburner to deliver posts. I've had it on my book blog for years and it reliably delivers posts every time one goes up.

There's a similar functionality on Blogger, although many on Blogger seem to use Feedburner. Something we will discuss in a future chapter is a free service that's very popular with book bloggers—Bloglovin'. Bloglovin' is a combination of feedreader and subscription. A link can be placed on your sidebar to allow your readers to subscribe to your blog through that method. Bloglovin' then delivers your readers a reminder every day that there are new posts from the blogs they've subscribed to.

The items mentioned above are the bare minimum for your sidebars. Personally, I like to throw all sorts of things up on my sidebar. If you are chatty on Twitter or Facebook, or involved in Pinterest, consider adding a Twitter stream widget, Facebook stream widget, or a Pinterest pinboard. Conversely, if you're never on Twitter, don't use a stream widget to highlight your absence. In terms of sidebar widgets, you want to accentuate the positives and hide the negatives. For example, if your blog only has 5 hits a day, don't put a hit counter on your sidebar. If your blog has a thousand hits a day, absolutely put that widget in a prominent spot!

It's considered good manners, and in fact many blog tour companies insist that you display a badge for their company on your sidebar if you host blog tours for them. Likewise, if you're a member of RWA (Romance Writers of America) or MWA (Mystery Writers of America), be sure to advertise your memberships.

By the way, this is easy to do. Just display the badges as a picture (in an image widget) and link to the URL of the applicable site. If you're unclear about hot-linking (linking to an external source) a graphic on your sidebar, see instructions in the Technical Help section at the end of this book.

Ultimately, it's your blog, but consider this analogy: your blog is your storefront. Think about the stores you frequent. Do you enjoy digging through mismatched piles of merchandise in a thrift store to locate what you want? Or do you prefer to easily find your next purchase? Some of us are bargain hunters and relish the hunt, but the majority of consumers will find an organized store more appealing. You need to do your best to project a professional front and be helpful to your readers.

Chapter 15 - Automating

AUTOMATING the dissemination of your blog posts is something that's frequently overlooked. You don't want to rely on people remembering which days you post, and you certainly don't want to rely on dumb luck for people to stumble upon your blog posts.

As mentioned previously, some readers prefer to subscribe to your RSS feed, whereas others like to have posts delivered to their inbox. Blog posts can even be disseminated to platforms like Twitter, Facebook, Google+ or LinkedIn, all of which can be automated.

This automation can occur in many ways, from plugins on your blog (like Jetpack on WordPress) to services like Dlvr.it (my personal favorite), to name a few. Jetpack is easy – just find the "Sharing" section of your "Settings" menu and go through the process of connecting each of your social media accounts to your blog. A quick note for those of you using Blogger – Dlvr.it is a good choice as it relies on the action of a service, not code on your site.

If you choose a service like Dlvr.it, sign into the service (https:// dlvr.it/), enter your RSS feed (and if you have to guess at this, it's likely your blog's URL with /feed/ at the end), then add each social media platform you want your posts delivered to. Make sure your posts go everywhere they can, without any work on your part. The last thing you want to do after slaving over a blog post is to remember everywhere you're supposed to send it.

You might be asking yourself, "What's an RSS feed?" You know that orange icon that kind of looks like a dot with radio waves going off to the side? That's the icon that connects to your RSS feed. Generally speaking, WordPress blogs have a feed URL of http://yourdomain.com/feed, but not always. And by the way, RSS means Really

Simple Syndication.

So now that we know what it is – what is it used for? The RSS feed is used to 'feed' your blog posts to other places. People can subscribe to your RSS feed and then read your blog in a feed reader, of which there are many. You can also use your RSS feed to allow your blog posts to be displayed as part of your Goodreads author profile or as part of your Amazon author profile. You can also 'feed' your blog posts to sites like BlogLovin' or Blog Catalog (a directory of blogs arranged according to content). We'll talk more about signing up to directories in our section on networking.

Whatever you choose, babysit it for a while to ensure that your posts go where they are meant to and most importantly, they look good. There are repeatedly problems with getting posts to automatically post to Facebook and look good. Facebook is constantly changing and that's likely the issue. Regardless of the cause, make sure that you are periodically looking at what posts to the various social media to make sure it doesn't look like something a toddler did.

Chapter 16 - Copyrighting the Blog Posts

THERE ARE STRONG feelings about copyrighting these days. From applying DRM encryption to your ebooks to copyrighting your blog posts, everyone has an opinion.

My opinion is that it's your choice whether or not you take any steps to stop plagiarism. I can explain various methods you can use to prevent copyright infringement or to identify it when it occurs, but you need to decide how important this is to you, and how much work you're willing to do.

Another thing to keep in mind is that ownership can be determined by the timestamp on your blog post. If you posted first, you own your work. Also, if you blog on either WordPress or Blogger (as well as several of the other platforms) they have a complaint mechanism that you can use if your copyright has been infringed on.

Although there are several services available to copyright your posts, I like using My Free Copyright (http://www.myfreecopyright.com/).

This service, as its name suggests, is free. Once you sign up for an account and confirm your choice, the site will start the process of backing up your content. You will be provided with some code to put on your blog and instructions on where to place it. Another similar service is DMCA (https://www.dmca.com/), which works in a similar fashion. If this is something you want to do, visit both sites to make an educated decision. Both services are fairly straightforward to set up.

Many authors also create a Google Alert for a unique sentence in each blog post to help police content theft. To sign up for Google

Alerts, log into your Google account and then go to https://www.google.com/alerts. You can create as many alerts as you choose. While we're on the topic of Google Alerts, I also have Alerts set up for my name and all my book titles to keep track of mentions of me and my books on the Internet. Something you might want to consider doing.

Chapter 17 - Using Amazon and other Affiliate Links

MOST AUTHORS have their books listed for sale on Amazon and other retailers, but rarely consider using affiliate links – either from Amazon or from other retailers – on their site. Because of my conversations with other authors, I realize that most don't understand the true power of using affiliate links.

Affiliate links allow authors to keep track of clicks on items on their sites as well as corresponding purchases. It's possible to keep track of clicks using Google Analytics or other stat programs – and we'll talk about that in the next chapter – but the power of affiliate links is being able to connect the clicks to the purchases.

First of all, let's talk about what an affiliate account is and then we'll move on to learn how to use it to provide valuable information.

Affiliate accounts are generally free, but need to be applied for. To track your books, you can get an affiliate account for almost every online bookseller. Amazon deals with their own affiliate program as does iTunes and Smashwords, but Kobo farms out this to a company called Rakuten Marketing. If your books are available on all these platforms, you will need to apply for four affiliate accounts if you want to be thorough. Since all these companies are American, if you live in a country other than the U.S., like I do, be prepared to supply tax information that they will find acceptable – in many cases an EIN. Since you are potentially going to earn money from your affiliate account, the various companies need to report your taxable income – hence the tax information.

Once your accounts are approved, you can create affiliate buy links for all your books. Some of the sites will allow you to create subsections of your account, allowing you to track clicks in various parts of your site.

Placing affiliate links on your site is as easy as hot-linking pictures or hyperlinking text. If this is something you struggle with, I have videos on how to do it in the Technical Help section.

Let's move on to the mechanics of an affiliate link. When someone clicks on an affiliate link on your site, the retailers will then track the actions of that reader. Anything they purchase via that retailer, be it a copy of one of your books or a new computer they look at after they purchase a copy of your book, will earn you a small amount of money. The actual amount of money is a percentage of the purchase price, and different products will pay you different rates.

It's nice to earn a small amount of money from the sale of your book, but what's even better is the information you get. Let's say your book is "How to Write a Mystery Novel" and you attach affiliate links to the mentions of your book on your site. After a few days you look at your affiliate dashboard – let's say on Amazon – and see that your links have had 100 clicks. When you look at what's purchased, you see that you haven't sold any copies of your book; in fact, people who clicked on your book ended up purchasing your competitor's book. You've sold 50 copies of your competitor's book! Not good, but this is information you can use.

You know that people are clicking on the links on your site, but when they get to Amazon they change their mind and purchase something else. Why? Look at your buy page on Amazon compared to your competitor's. Are the prices significantly different? In other words, have you priced yourself out of your market? Is your competitor's blurb more compelling? Does it do a better job of selling the book than yours? Ask your friends to compare and be your second set of eyes. If you find something that needs to change, then change it and sit back and see if your stats tell you that you've made a difference in your readers' behavior. See if more of the clicks result in sales of YOUR book.

If you choose to use Affiliate links on your site, it's imperative that you read the chapter on FTC rules. You don't want to end up on the wrong side of the FTC!

In the next section, we're going to spend some more time on stats.

I LOVE stats, but I'm well aware that they can become addictive. Affiliate information, like other forms of stats, should be used as a tool, not the reason you didn't get any writing done.

CHAPTER 18 - UNDERSTANDING STATS

AS I MENTIONED in the previous section, we need to spend some time talking about stats. As a science graduate with a major in Genetics, I've come to love stats. I don't 'think' things happen on my blogs – I 'know' they happen. The reason I know this is that I pay attention to the stats on my blogs.

The two most common methods to collect stats on your blog are Google Analytics and if you have a WordPress.com or WordPress.org blog, you have access to Jetpack stats. If you have a Blogger blog, it comes with its own stats program, and has the ability to have Google Analytics installed quite easily.

If you've looked at the plugins available on WordPress.org, you're aware that there are quite a few choices for measuring your stats. The main concern for a stats program is that it only measures human hits. In other words, it keeps track of humans who visit your blog, not spam or non-human visits. This seems like an obvious point to make – I mean, really, who cares how many spam bots visit your blog and leave an annoying little comment behind for you to delete? Interestingly, there are stats programs that count humans and non-humans. An example is the stats program found on Blogger. I'm not sure why the Blogger stats program (and others) count non-human hits, but it's certainly misleading. I can't count the number of people who get a rude wake-up call when they install Google Analytics on their Blogger blog and see that their hits are a fraction of what the Blogger stat program says.

So, yes, there are quite a few choices to measure the stats on your blog, but I suggest using a combination of Google Analytics and Jetpack stats (if you have access to it). Before we start with our discussion, if you're unclear as to how to put Google Analytics on either your WordPress or Blogger blog, I've created videos that walk you through this process and links to these videos can be found in the Technical Help section at the back of this book.

The two stats programs I recommend have different strengths, yet are similar in many ways. I use Google Analytics to look at where my audience is (geographical location), time spent on my blog, bounce rate, and what type of device my readers use to access my site. I use Jetpack for everything else.

Let's start with Google Analytics. At first glance Google Analytics is an overwhelming collection of numbers and percentages. That's why I focus on a small number of figures – I find that I don't get overwhelmed with information that I either don't care about or can't use. When you go to your Google Analytics dashboard you are presented with an overview of a day, a week or a month's worth of summary numbers. We're going to start our discussion with geographical location. To find those numbers, look on the left side of your screen for Geo and click on the arrow to expand the section and then click on Location.

I'm very interested in where my audience is physically located. I think the normal reaction with blogs is that our audience is likely from our own country. Yet because our site is available on the Internet, it's open to the world. You might be surprised to discover that a large percentage of your hits come from a different country than the one in which you live. I know that India and other Asian countries are considered to be emerging markets for bloggers. In fact, I have one blog – my book blog – that receives almost 50% of its traffic from India.

Why do we care where our audience is located? The first reason would be to help us understand who our readers are, and secondly, to better focus our promotions. Let's use my blog that has a lot of its audience in India as an example. If I want to do a Facebook ad that targets my blog's demographics, but I don't include India in the choices, I may not be targeting my readers. Likewise, if I want to expand the reach of my blog using Google AdWords, I can include countries where I know my readership is low. Let's use the example of a giveaway. Since I live in Canada, I'm frequently excluded from a lot of giveaways and other promotions so this is a topic dear to my heart. If

I know that the majority of my audience is from countries other than the U.S. and I offer a giveaway that excludes these countries, I'm likely to alienate my readers. Something to think about...

Let's move on to the time spent on site and the bounce rate. It seems that everyone and their dog is willing to spout an opinion about how long your blog posts should be and whether or not you should have a magazine format for your site. I feel that these decisions should be made on the basis of your stats.

First of all, we need to locate two important stats: Average Session Duration and Bounce Rate. Both are found on the dashboard or the first thing you see when you log in to Google Analytics.

The Average Session Duration is the average amount of time spent on the site. Look at that number, set a timer for that amount of time and read something until the timer goes off. That will give you a general feel for how much your readers are reading. If the average is over a minute, you're actually keeping their attention for a good amount of time! But...I've read quite a few posts suggesting that authors write 1,500 to 2,000 words for every post. Can you read 2,000 words in a minute or less? Although there are reasons other than stats for making longer posts, in this section we're focusing on stats. If you want to create longer posts for other reasons, yet your stats say your readers are only reading for 30 seconds, make sure you include the content you want your readers to read near the beginning of the post.

Let's expand on that to talk about magazine format blogs. This format is one where only an excerpt shows of the post. The reader must then click on a button or text link to read the entirety of the post. I'm not a huge fan of this format for authors as I feel that readers of blogs are innately lazy and more often than not, they don't click to read more, they just move on. Keep in mind that every audience is different and generalities are dangerous to make, but your stats will tell you what's happening on your site.

To answer this question, we want to look at not only the time readers spend on our site, but also look at what's called bounce rate. Bounce Rate can be defined as "the percentage of visitors to a website who navigate away from the site after viewing only one page." Bounce rate is a number that needs to be taken into context. If your landing page (the page people land on when they type in your direct URL) is made up of blog posts that are displayed in their entirety, then viewing one page isn't a bad thing. However, if your landing page is simply a welcome with a short blurb about you and your books, losing your audience after viewing this one page isn't ideal. It means they aren't reading any of your blog posts.

Before you have a panic attack – as I did when I first figured out what 'bounce rate' was – you need to put these numbers into context. First, figure out where your audience begins their visit to your site and then look at bounce rate. To add a bit more context, Google Analytics will also tell you the average number of pages viewed. So do they start one place and quickly move elsewhere? In a previous chapter, we talked about the various strategies to link posts to one another and to other sources. This information is applicable to our conversation about bounce rates. I feel that the longer you can keep a reader on your blog, the more likely you are to get a sale or a subscription to your site.

The last item on my list for Google Analytics is the type of device readers use to view the site. Are they reading your site on a desktop computer or a mobile device like a tablet or cellphone? Have a peek at the section under the term "Audience," followed by "Mobile" on your Google Analytics account. These numbers might surprise you. We now know that more and more people access the internet using a mobile device so Google strongly encourages us to have a mobile responsive website. What's a mobile responsive website? A site is "mobile responsive" when it looks good on all types of devices and in fact will change structure to suit viewing on smaller screens. (More information on mobile responsive in Chapter 6.)

Frankly, a lot of authors I work with say, "I don't have a tablet or a phone and I'm sure my readers are only looking at my site on a desktop computer." I then challenge them to look at their stats. Some are right, but others are quite surprised by the percentage of readers who view their site using a cellphone or tablet. Every audience is different, but just like the physical location of your audience is important, understanding how they view what you create is also important.

Let's move on to what you can learn from Jetpack stats found on WordPress. All of the information we will talk about viewing on Jetpack stats can also be found on Google Analytics but I like the presentation on Jetpack better.

If you look at your full screen view of Jetpack stats it has 6 sections that we will discuss. The most obvious section is the bar graph that fills the top area. This bar graph can be changed to see stats by days, weeks, or months. This section (like the other sections we will talk about) has a summary link in the upper right corner. I often find looking at the summaries of each of these areas is more helpful than looking at one day's worth of stats as it gives you a wider view.

Although it's lovely to know how many people visited your blog each day, we want to look at the details of these visits to get actionable information.

Moving down and to the left, find the box labeled Referrers. This is where your traffic is coming from (if they didn't directly enter your URL). In this section, you'll find where your reader clicked on something to lead them to you. I use this area to find people who have linked to me and to see what kind of traffic I garner from my social media accounts. If you've never looked at this information before, you might be surprised by where your traffic originates. Just because you have a lot of retweets on Twitter doesn't mean readers come to your blog. This section will help you to understand how effective your social media accounts are in drawing traffic to your blog.

The section below Referrers is Search Engine Terms. I don't pay a lot of attention to this area, but I'm interested in determining what people are searching for when they find my sites. I'll look at the results every couple of weeks. Honestly, I'm often entertained by what words or phrases people use to find my sites. Look at your results and see if you can see some interesting search terms.

The box below Search Engine Terms is Subscriptions. This will tell you how many people use the WordPress subscription functionality to subscribe to or comment on your blog. To see who has subscribed to your blog in this fashion, just click on the link and you can see a list of names.

Tech Hint: If you have set up Feedburner to manage your blog subscriptions, those subscribers will not show up in this location.

Next, look for the box labeled Top Posts & Pages toward the top right of the screen. This will help you understand where people start their reading journey on your blog. It's likely that a large number of the entries are for "Home page/Archives." That means that people have clicked on your direct URL to get to your site. If they've clicked on a direct link to a specific blog post from a FB post or a Twitter link you'll see that indicated by numbers beside specific posts. Not only can you use this to discover which are your most popular posts – and give your readers more similar content – you can also make generalizations about starting points on your blog.

As an example, on my business blog I created a blog post with screenshots that walk people through the process of adding affiliate links to their blog posts. This post is almost two-years-old, but it gets at least one hit every day – and most days it gets 20 or 30 hits.

Lastly, the box further down on the right is labeled Clicks. This area tells you what's been clicked on within your site and how many times. As I mentioned in the previous section on Affiliate links, stats can tell you clicks on buy links, but only affiliate links can tell you clicks vs. sales. If you have things you want your readers to click on that aren't sales links, your Clicks section will help you understand that type of traffic.

One major point to keep in mind as you wade through all this information is that your blog stats are only a fraction of the story. For example, you have no idea how many people subscribe to your blog using your RSS and their feedreader. If you send out blog posts to readers by email, they don't usually count as hits on your blog as the email often contains your whole post and readers have no need to visit your blog to read that post.

If you have your Facebook page set up so that your FB friends can view your blog posts on FB, they don't count as hits. If you've shared your posts on your LinkedIn activity feed, or Goodreads account, those readers don't count on your hits. These are just a few examples that don't register on your blog stats. So…for the days that you post on your blog and you don't see many hits, please don't panic – you're only looking at a fraction of the whole picture.

Let's conclude this section of Stats with some final thoughts. Stats should help you understand a lot about your blog and your readers' behavior. I hope you use it to make changes where necessary to your site or content. I also hope you take all the information you gather with a grain of salt and sense of humor. Although I know that I could spend hours analyzing the stats for my sites, I don't. And I don't suggest you do either. Use them as a tool to guide you, but not as an obsession to occupy time that you should be writing.

CHAPTER 19 - FTC STATEMENT

THE FTC is the Federal Trade Commission, an American government organization tasked with ensuring that companies carry out fair business practices. Where this relates to authors is with respect to the books we receive free for review and any money made from affiliate or other advertising. If you don't accept free books, or receive any advertising money from authors or publishers or affiliates, you can ignore this section. Also, if you live outside of the U.S., you can ignore this section (mostly).

The FTC has set rather complicated regulations in place regarding the posting of thoughts on products that were obtained for the purpose of reviewing. The vast majority of reviewers don't get paid to review books. We receive books for free from authors and/or publishers. Because of this, the FTC requires this fact be stated. For several years, it was assumed by many reviewers that a statement to that fact placed on the blog's sidebar was sufficient to satisfy the FTC ruling.

As has recently been posted on several sources, it's now suggested that American book bloggers/reviewers state clearly at the beginning of their post that they've received the book being discussed in the post for free in exchange for an honest review. If there are affiliate links in the post, state that as well. A single statement in the sidebar is not considered visible enough.

So, is the FTC going to go after every book blogger or author who reviews a couple of handfuls of books each year or gets $10 or $12 in affiliate money each year? Not likely. It's better to be safe than sorry, however. By placing a statement at the beginning of each review post, your butt is covered.

You'll notice that the FTC is an American entity and as such, can only enforce their rules on American bloggers/authors. I'm Canadian and until recently felt it unnecessary to put a disclosure on any of my blogs. While doing the research for this book, I discovered that it is possible for the FTC to go after American authors or American publishers rather than a blogger from another country. Because I don't want the possibility of the American government going after American authors or publishers due to the fact that I read and review their books, I'm now going to put the disclaimer on all posts related to receiving free books and those that contain an affiliate link. I suggest that you do the same.

CHAPTER 20 - MAINTENANCE OF YOUR BLOG

BACKING UP and updating your blog are two functions that everyone talks about, but as a troubleshooter who comes in when something bad happens to a blog, I know these two subjects aren't give enough attention!

Let's talk about backing up first. All blogs, regardless of platform need to be backed up. Yes, I know that Blogger and WordPress.com do backups and safeguard your content. They also have rules that must be followed. If the rules aren't followed, they shut down your blog and all of your content is lost.

I'm a rule follower. I know not everyone is and there are a lot of authors who haven't read the rules they're supposed to follow. If you do run afoul of the rules and get shut down, having a backup saves your content and lets you start up again elsewhere.

Backing up your blog can be done on almost all platforms. One method is to take an export of your content on a regular basis and keep it in a safe place – your hard drive or a zip drive – somewhere away from your blog (i.e.: Not stored on your hosting in case something happens to your hosting). An export can be taken from Blogger, Wordpress.com and Wordpress.org. On Blogger, look at "Settings" and then "Other." On both WordPress.com and WordPress.org go to "Users" and choose "Export" and then choose "All Content." If this seems intimidating to you, I've created a YouTube video that walks you through this process. Please see the Technical Help section at the end of this book for a link to the video.

WordPress.org offers a huge number of plugins that will backup your blog. The ones I prefer will operate on a preset schedule (so I don't have to remember) and sends a copy of my content to my Dropbox. Plugins that backup to your hosting account can result in less available space. Also, if you lose or move your hosting, you may forget to take your backup files with you. As I mentioned previously, my preference is Updraft – a free plugin. But have a look through the choices and find one that works for you. Whatever you decide, just make sure you do something!

Updating is another issue that isn't given enough attention in my experience. It is essential that you keep everything on your blog up-to-date. Since this function is done for you on Blogger and WordPress.com blogs, my comments are aimed at the owners of WordPress.org blogs. Frequently, hackers use security 'holes' that exist in out-of-date plugins or versions of WordPress to gain access to your site. Because of this, it is imperative that everything is kept current. It's not uncommon for free plugins to be abandoned by their developers. The little prompt I get to update plugins gets me to act, but I was having trouble remembering to check for out-of-date plugins. I now have a calendar reminder every 4 months that prompts me to have a peek.

The method isn't important, just keep everything up-to-date.

I need to have one last word on the security side of your site. Research shows us that a secure password prevents the vast majority of hackers from getting into your blog. Let's face it, if someone wants in, they will get in – see Sony as a good example. The average author site isn't a serious target for a hacker in most cases. Right now WordPress is trying to strongly encourage secure login passwords on its sites. Their version of a strong password is pretty ugly! It's a seemingly random collection of small letters, capital letters, numbers, and symbols. Definitely something you would have trouble remembering. To deviate for a second, I have a program on my computer called 1Password that retains all the passwords I tell it to. I only need to remember one password – the one that controls its access. I strongly suggest you have a program like that to help you use and generate strong passwords.

At a bare minimum, use passwords that are only meaningful to you and don't contain anything predictable. Don't use your house address, your cat's name, or your birthdate. And for heaven sake, don't use abcde12345 – yes, some people do. I suggest a password that's at least 10 characters long and a combination of capitals, lowercase, numbers, and weird symbols (like ^ and ~, not * and !)

Before you leave this chapter, I want you to log onto your blog and make sure a method of back up is in place and operational. If there isn't, first take an export of your blog so you have that on the hard drive of your computer. Secondly, if you have a <u>WordPress.org</u> site, choose a backup plugin and put it in place and set it to automatically backup.

Once that's done, I want you to set up a reminder system to make sure your site stays up-to-date and secure. At a bare minimum, you log into and observe your site once a week. Any plugins that indicate an available update (by a number in a circle on the menu beside the word "Plugin" on your dashboard or by the text link saying "Update Now") should be updated.

I also suggest that you backup your blog at least once a month. Set a reminder to check your blog once every 4 to 6 months for out-of-date/abandoned plugins. To do this just click on the 'View Details' link for each plugin and make sure it's been updated recently. If it hasn't, choose a different plugin that performs the same function, but is up-to-date. These steps will keep your blog current.

Chapter 21 - Networking AKA Finding an Audience

EVER SINCE I created The Book Blogger List (http://bookblog-gerlist.com/), I got a lot of questions from authors as well as bloggers about networking – expanding their reach and finding an audience.

By having a well-optimized blog with posts added on a regular basis, you should show up on Google pretty quickly. Although Google searches will bring you a certain amount of traffic, it's a good plan to go out and find some like-minded bloggers or authors. I certainly don't suggest that you sit on your duff and wait for people to come visiting – I suggest a more proactive approach.

As I said earlier, creating an audience on a blog is akin to making friends in Kindergarten. You know… "Hi, my name is Barb, will you be my friend?" Since I'm making friends as an adult, I might say, "Hi, my name is Barb and I read Regency Romance. I love the books you read! We should chat about books!" Although I say you should find authors or other bloggers, I find that authors preferably network with other authors – there's a comfort zone there. I encourage you to find readers and friends for your blogs in a variety of places – not just with fellow authors!

To start your networking, you need to find authors and other bloggers with whom to have a virtual conversation. The most basic step to this is to visit and leave comments on other blogs. Find some book bloggers who read a similar genre to you – people who have common interests to yours. Leave a comment with a nice compliment on their latest post. For example, "Hi! My name is Barb and this is my first visit to your blog. Thanks for sharing your thoughts on (book title). Looks like I read similar books to you and I'm always looking for something new to read. I'll be back." If you have an interest in horses or dogs, look to blogs that would be of interest to you. Likewise if you like to talk about being retired military. Whatever the topic that interests you, the Internet has lots of people out there with similar interests.

Most comment systems force you to list your name, email address, and blog URL to leave a comment. If you are sincere, bloggers/authors will come visiting. They may not visit after your first visit, but if you keep visiting them, they will visit you. I've found some of my best on-line friends by visiting and commenting on their blogs.

Although this point might be common sense to some, it needs to be spelled out – when you leave a comment, don't self-promote. For example, if you leave a comment on a book blogger post where they've reviewed a book, DON'T SAY: "Hi My name is Barb and I write books similar to the one you've just reviewed, yet much better. I simply must send you a copy of my book to read so you can appreciate what great literature is really like." You may think I'm being funny with that example, but sadly, I see that sort of comment frequently on my book blog, and it doesn't make me want to read that author's book!

Secondly, use social media to find fellow authors and book bloggers. Pinterest, Twitter and Facebook as well as Instagram are favorite hangouts of book bloggers. The more you talk about books the more people will join in the conversation. A tweet I post occasionally says: "I have my latte and my comfy chair…what should I be reading?" The book recommendations I get from that tweet are amazing!

> **Tech Hint:** In order to make good use of your blog posts, don't be afraid to 're-purpose' them every so often. It's not uncommon to tweet a link or Facebook a link to an older post to bring attention to it again. Blog posts can be found years after they're created either because you've drawn attention to it or because they are easily found on a Google search.

You should look for an audience anywhere you can find people with similar interests. That means to expand your reach beyond fellow authors and book bloggers. You may find friends who have blogs that talk about whatever interest you have in common. If your interest is in brewing beer, by all means, search for fellow brewers who blog about their interests. If your interests lie with crafting, likewise, search out people who blog about similar topics.

Authors commonly guest post on each other's blogs or on book bloggers' blogs, believing they'll make new friends/readers by doing so. This may be true to a certain extent, but I'm not a huge fan of guest posting as I feel that it isn't done properly. There's only a benefit to the guest poster if the blog they are posting to has high traffic numbers and a potentially interested audience. If this isn't the case, guest posting can be a lot of work with little return on investment.

Lastly, try some memes. These are group activities you can join and are a great way to find people to follow and follow back. Instructions and a discussion of Memes can be found in the next chapter. Find a few that sound fun and join!

CHAPTER 22 - BEING MORE SOCIAL

I THINK one of the best things about having a blog is the social aspect. I love chatting about books with people from all over the world. In my "real" life I don't always meet people who read what I do, and I certainly don't have access to people from a variety of countries and cultures as I do online.

I like being part of the various groups. I can pop in and chat and then return to my regular life. As I've said previously, a tweet I send out periodically says, "I have my latte, my comfy chair, and my book. What are you reading?" I love the answers I get! So many are book suggestions! For the same reason, I like popping in to my various groups or participating in a meme to catch up on bookish news and maybe find a new book to read.

There are so many ways of being more social with a blog. From bookish groups, to weekly memes, the list seems endless. I'm going to briefly describe a selection to get you started on finding ways to be social that might work for you. Remember, since I'm a stats geek, the phrase "works for you" can be defined as traffic coming to your blog from these various sites or memes.

One point to keep in mind as you work on being more social, things change quickly in the blogosphere. Over the space of writing this book, one of the sites I typically use as my go-to networking site closed up shop. Below, find some suggestions of sites you can explore, but don't hesitate to use a Google search to keep your eyes open for new sites to join and experience as they grow.

Blogaholic—Social Network for Bloggers

Blogaholic (http://www.blogaholicnetwork.com/) is a social networking place for bloggers, which you can join for free and find some friends. It's been around for 4 or 5 years.

Although Blogaholic doesn't look very busy at the time of this writing, there's still activity. You can list your blog, join groups and even more interesting, you can find a listing of blog hops and weekly memes.

This site isn't restricted to book/author blogs; there are categories for a wide variety of blogs. This allows you to find people who blog about a variety of subjects—and it also allows you to follow more passions other than bookish ones! Again, this is a site you can join and make friends. Just because you have an author blog doesn't mean you aren't interested in following some photography blogs or maybe some recipe/food blogs.

Blog Catalog

Blog Catalog (note the spelling) (http://www.blogcatalog.com/) is a site you can join for free and list your blog. Like Blogaholic, this site isn't restricted to certain types of blogs, so you'll find all sorts of blogs to read! Once you list some information about you and your blog, your feed will be pulled and your posts will be displayed for the curious.

I don't see a lot of traffic from this listing, but I do see some. Since it's free, I suggest setting up an account and listing your blog as well as putting a badge on your sidebar.

It's possible to have your blog advertised on this site for a fee. For more details, see the site.

Blog Nation

Blog Nation (http://www.blognation.com/) is a relatively new site open to all bloggers. According to the description on the site:

Blog Nation is a comprehensive network of blogs that seeks to give recognition and viewership to the millions of fantastic blogs currently on the Internet. Their aim is both to help users gain exposure and allow viewers to discover new and exciting blogs that spark their unique interests.

According to their home page, they have more than 15,000 blogs listed with all sorts of interests represented. They will pull your blog feed and display your posts to their audience.

They also have a selection of cool badges that fit nicely on site sidebars. Again, it's free and worth listing your blog there.

Bloglovin'

Bloglovin' (http://www.bloglovin.com/) is a blog reader program. For those of you familiar with the late Google Reader, Bloglovin' is a really nice version of that service. Once you set up your profile, you can choose blogs to follow.

The reader platform is open—easy to read. There's also an app for your smartphone that will allow you to read the latest blog posts on your way to work if you take a train, or perhaps at the gym while you're running the treadmill!

You can also create a badge for your sidebar that will allow readers to sign up to follow your blog on Bloglovin'.

Weekly Blog Memes

Weekly Blog Memes are another social opportunity that bloggers can take advantage of. If you remember, I mentioned using memes to help attract attention to your posts in an earlier chapter. Simply put, they are an activity—usually weekly and on a specific day of the week. You create a post on your blog, add the graphic from the blog hosting the meme, link to that blog, and in most cases add your name/blog name and URL to a Linky list. Once that's done, you go visiting. Visit everyone on the list, make sure you follow them in some fashion, and make some friends; comment, share the post, or invite the blogger to visit your blog.

Weekly Memes are fun and a great way of not only adding content to your blog, but also networking and building a following. When I first started my blog, posting memes and following links was how I met some of my best online friends—people who love books as much as I do, and people who read what I read.

Although weekly memes are more common on hobby blogs, there are a lot that are applicable specifically to authors. But honestly, there's nothing wrong with joining a book blogger meme – I mean, you do read, don't you? There's a great meme that I used to play on Wednesdays where we would list books we were eagerly anticipating. Nothing better than chatting about books, I say.

The one I mentioned in a previous chapter is Wordless Wednesday, but there are lots of other types of memes. There are memes around all sorts of activities – the key is to make some friends while doing something that interests you. Maybe your interests are following writing prompts, creating flash fiction, or even posting pictures of your cat. Quite frankly, if you write racy romance, you might want to participate in a Man Candy Meme. That might be an ideal place to find readers of what you write!

The important detail to participating in a meme is to not only put content on your blog, but find a blog that has what we call a Linky List – code that lists the group of like-minded bloggers who also participate in the meme. They will enter their blog name and direct URL to their post in the Linky List and then go and visit everyone on the list. The Linky List is the important part of this activity. You want to be found. You want people who are participating in the activity to find you. You also want to have a list of blogs to visit and find potential friends.

Lastly, in terms of being more social, your blog post feed can be connected to your Amazon author page as well as your Goodreads author profile very easily. That way, anyone who is looking at your books on your Amazon Author Page can see your latest blog posts and people who are friends of yours on Goodreads can see your blog posts on their news feed. Additionally, your followers may be notified every time you post your blog. There are lots of opportunities to find friends and nurture friendships.

Conclusion

WE HAVE reached the end of Blogging for Authors. I hope you've learned a lot. In fact, I hope that I have changed the way you look at blogging. My greatest wish is that you are now eager to approach blogging as a method of communication with your readers and community with greater confidence.

As I promised, I want to provide a coupon for 50% off my Word-Press for Beginner's course that is offered through Udemy. If you are reading this book as an ebook, click here. (https://www.udemy.com/wordpress-for-beginners-2016-perfect-for-authors-bloggers/?couponCode=BloggingForAuthorsReaders) If you are reading this book in paperback, contact me at sugarbeatbc@gmail.com so that I can email you a code. My course is specifically aimed at beginner authors and is meant to be non-technical in its instruction.

Please visit one of my blogs and say hi. I'm always around and happy to answer questions. Subscribe to my business blog and get little gems of information in your inbox. As you can well imagine, I love chatting about books. I've included my links at the end of this book. Please follow me, and friend me, and chat with me about books! Share your thoughts with me about this book, and if you feel inclined, please post a review of your thoughts wherever you feel comfortable doing so. Good choices are Goodreads and Amazon, but so is your blog. Invite me over to say hi and I'll help you promote your post.

Technical Help

WELCOME TO THE SECTION of this book where I explain some of the technical aspects of blogging. Over the years, I've come to realize that manipulating WordPress or Blogger comes quite easily to some, and not so easily to others. The idea behind this section of the book is to supply you with pointers to help you step up your game, or if you're struggling, to explain some of the sticky points of the two major platforms.

The current list of videos and links available on YouTube is listed below. All of my videos can be found on my YouTube channel—Bakerview Consulting. If you're reading the paperback version of this book or your e-reader doesn't allow clicking on external links, simply go to http://youtube.com and search for "Bakerview Consulting." You will find all the videos listed there. Feel free to work your way through the videos you feel will be helpful to you.

Videos

WordPress Instruction

How to Customize your Dashboard and other Workspaces on WordPress:

https://www.youtube.com/watch?v=PdbevOSVS-I

How to Insert & Size Pictures in a WordPress Post or Page:

https://www.youtube.com/watch?v=MJZ9tLveX7s

Making Pictures Behave in WordPress Posts or Pages:
https://www.youtube.com/watch?v=jgmKewZbtcw

How to Attach a Link to a Picture in a WordPress Post/Page:
https://www.youtube.com/watch?v=581QZAlMrFU

How to Use Tiled Galleries in a WordPress Post:
https://www.youtube.com/watch?v=IHWXh3kKeho

How to use Different or Alternate Sources of Pictures
for your WordPress Post or Page:
https://www.youtube.com/watch?v=pETRYZLr4vI

Formatting Text in a WordPress Post or Page:
https://www.youtube.com/watch?v=CGQuJsNq5Zs

How to Put HTML or iFrame code in a Widget in WordPress:
https://www.youtube.com/watch?v=AsHrrZawe9g

How to Embed a YouTube Video in a WordPress Post:
https://www.youtube.com/watch?v=Fhjoy6MzMvE

How to Insert a YouTube Video in a WordPress Post:
https://www.youtube.com/watch?v=Fhjoy6MzMvE

How to Edit Pictures Using the Editing Functions on WP:
https://www.youtube.com/watch?v=bCgx2oeEswQ

How to Create HTML Code to Put Follow Icons on the Sidebar in WP:
https://www.youtube.com/watch?v=dxqDti89gco

How to Add Google Analytics to a WordPress blog:
https://www.youtube.com/watch?v=L0iqu6ievQw

How to Embed Hyperlinks in a WordPress Post or Page:
https://www.youtube.com/watch?v=ptp34EU44Mc

Videos About Amazon and Your Blog:
How to Add Amazon Affiliate Links to a Post/Page in WordPress:
https://www.youtube.com/watch?v=d3625R0yfJ0

Why Use Amazon Affiliate Links on your Blog:
https://www.youtube.com/watch?v=J7n4p5c7VGs

Blogger Instruction:
How to Link Pictures on a Blogger Post or Page:
https://www.youtube.com/watch?v=eHxhDzbGnaQ&spfreload=10

Manipulating Images in Blogger Posts or Pages:
https://www.youtube.com/watch?v=BUZY0oOC4sM

How to Put an Image on the Sidebar of a Blogger Blog:
https://www.youtube.com/watch?v=7Ywjvg08wTM

How to Put HTML or iFrame code on the Sidebar of a Blogger Blog:
https://www.youtube.com/watch?v=jwtO-6-YXHM

How to Format Text in a Blogger Post:
https://www.youtube.com/watch?v=huNpD9-PKSo

How to Insert a YouTube Video in a Blogger Post:
https://www.youtube.com/watch?v=zXp-lI5B628

How to Put Code on the Sidebar of a Blogger Blog:
https://www.youtube.com/watch?v=jwtO-6-YXHM

How to Put an Image on the Sidebar of a Blogger Blog:
https://www.youtube.com/watch?v=yg7QAF6j1t0

How to Add Google Analytics to a Blogger Blog:
https://www.youtube.com/watch?v=Ific90gGJrg

Tech Tidbits for All Bloggers:
How to Put a Signature at the Bottom of a Blog Post:
https://www.youtube.com/watch?v=MAheCmM887s

The Cheater's Way of Creating HTML Using a Blog Post:
https://www.youtube.com/watch?v=c6jWVV9BWYQ

How to Create Export Files to Serve as Backup Files on WP and Blogger:
https://www.youtube.com/watch?v=E_Nl468dJCk

* * *

Because bloggers repeatedly tell me that some tech subjects are difficult for them, further explanations and reminders about links to the videos are listed below.

* * *

Customization of the WordPress Dashboard

One complaint I hear over and over from people just starting out on WordPress is that it's overwhelming. There's too much information to look at. I honestly think some bloggers choose Blogger because of its simplistic and uncluttered workspace. A similar situation can be created on WordPress. For a visual walkthrough of customizing your workspace see the YouTube video here:

https://www.youtube.com/watch?v=PdbevOSVS-I

Pretty much every screen in WordPress can be customized. If you look in the upper right corner of most screens you will see a "Screen Options" button. Click on that button and a screen will drop down, presenting you with check boxes that will allow you to modify what is or isn't on that particular screen. Some people need detail that others do not. Go through the screens for your WordPress blog and customize them to suit your workflow.

You can also customize the colors of the various parts of the backside or dashboard of your WordPress blog. From the menu bar on the left hand side, click on User and then My Profile and adjust the color to something that suits you. Change it once or change it with the seasons!

Analytics

There are quite a few ways to monitor the stats on your blog. There's always a lot of chatter about the stats program on Blogger. Blogger users are often disappointed if they move to WordPress and their traffic stats aren't as high as on Blogger. The stats program on Blogger counts hits in a different way than other programs. It counts human and non-human hits, which results in Blogger users often having an inflated opinion of how many "people" are visiting their blog. Most stats programs only track the hits from real people. You can well imagine the inflation of the numbers if non-human hits were counted.

I have one site that typically gets more than 1,000 spam hits a day! If you're curious about this, a Google search will point you in the direction of quite a few articles on the subject.

The most common way to measure stats on blogs is by using Google Analytics. On WordPress, the Jetpack Stats plugin runs a close second. Both can be easily installed and supply bloggers with a great overall view of who is visiting their blog.

On my WordPress blogs, I like to use both types of monitors as they have different strengths. WordPress does a great job of keeping track of clicks and what words are used in a Google search. Google Analytics does a great job of telling you the geographic origin of your visitors and how long on average they spend on your blog. For details on how to install both types of stats, I've created a video for Word-Press: https://www.youtube.com/watch?v=L0iqu6ievQw

and for Blogger:

https://www.youtube.com/watch?v=Ific90gGJrg

Formatting Text

Once you have the text of your post or page in place, it's important to understand the options available to you in terms of formatting. Readers of electronic sources—such as blogs—tend to have short attention spans. You can choose whether or not to cater to this. If you decide to cater to it there are a number of easy things you can do to your blog posts to encourage these readers to keep going.

• Create short paragraphs that are separated with a quote from the upcoming paragraph.
• Create subheadings.
• Use pictures to separate the paragraphs.

I've created a video on formatting in WordPress:
https://www.youtube.com/watch?v=CGQuJsNq5Zs

and one for Blogger:

https://www.youtube.com/watch?v=huNpD9-PKSo

I hope these suggestions will show you some formatting options you weren't familiar with and give you some ideas to change the look of your next blog post.

Creating an Export

As we discussed previously, I encourage you to have a program that regularly and automatically backs up your blog without you having to think about it. The paranoid side of me thinks it's a good idea to spontaneously create backups of your blog, especially before you update your plugins, if you're operating a self-hosted WordPress blog. I have a video that leads you through the steps involved here:

https://www.youtube.com/watch?v=E_Nl468dJCk

As you'll learn in the video, it's as simple as taking an export of your blog contents. Is it the best backup you can have—NO, but it's certainly better than nothing! What you'll get from an export is all of your content. You won't generate an exact replica of your blog in terms of its organization – that you'll have to recreate – but as I said, it's better than losing all of your work.

For those of you with a Blogger or WordPress.com blog, you can assume correctly that both of those will maintain and backup your blog. What can happen, however is Blogger/WordPress.com can decide to shut down your blog if you aren't following their rules. If that happens, it's generally without much warning, and all your content can be lost. For that reason, I think Blogger and WordPress.com bloggers need to keep an export of their posts on their hard drive as a little piece of insurance.

Akismet

Akismet is the program many bloggers use to deal with spam. There are many plugins or programs available to deal with spam, but this is the most common one.

Let's clear up a few misconceptions. Spam happens. To a certain extent, I see spam as a sign of a healthy blog. If the automated programs used to leave spam on your blog can't find you, then what hope do you have that readers will find you? Is spam annoying? Yes! Your job as a blogger is to ensure the spam that lands on your blog doesn't appear to your readers. That's where Akismet comes in. The role of this plugin is to segregate spam into a specific folder or leave it for you to moderate.

Akismet is an intelligent program. If a comment is left for you to moderate and you determine that it's spam, mark it as such—don't just trash it. That will help you in the future.

Next point – do you have to delete spam? I think you do. Not because it will cause harm to your blog, but ultimately it will take up space – space it doesn't deserve to have access to! So, take a few moments every so often to dump the spam from your blog.

Images or Graphics in Blog Posts or Pages

In my experience, there's nothing like trying to insert a picture into a post or page to make even the most experienced blogger swear like a trucker!

In the first video on this subject – How to Insert & Size Pictures in a WordPress Post or Page:

https://www.youtube.com/watch?v=MJZ9tLveX7s

I demonstrate the basic method of putting a picture into a Word-Press Post or Page, and how to place it on the left, center, or right of the space with the words wrapping, if applicable.

The next video, appropriately called Making Pictures Behave in WordPress Posts or Pages:

https://www.youtube.com/watch?v=jgmKewZbtcw

covers a few hints on getting pictures to stay where you put them and also how to create an organized display of pictures in a post or page.

The next video called How to use Different or Alternate Sources of Pictures for your WordPress Post or Page:

https://www.youtube.com/watch?v=pETRYZLr4vI

covers alternative sources of pictures for your WordPress post or page. As book bloggers, we often use cover graphics from Amazon, Goodreads, or from the author. We need to think outside of the box sometimes.

Previous videos cover using a graphic from the media library, and this one covers grabbing pictures from the hard drive of your computer as well as linking to an external source. This may not be something you do on a regular basis, but it's good to have options.

The last video in the series of dealing with images on WordPress is called: How to Attach a Link to a Picture in a WordPress Post/Page:

https://www.youtube.com/watch?v=581QZAlMrFU

People like to click on pictures—especially with so many people reading our blogs on mobile devices. They tap on everything. I frequently link cover graphics to buy pages on Amazon, so if someone clicks or taps, they can be encouraged to buy a copy of the book they're interested in. There are a lot of other examples of why we would attach a link to a graphic – what's called "hotlinking" pictures.

Not to leave out Blogger users, I've created a couple of videos walking through various actions on that platform.

Manipulating Images in Blogger Posts or Pages:

https://www.youtube.com/watch?v=BUZY0oOC4sM

describes how to put a picture in place, how to move it around, and how to change the size.

How to Link Pictures on a Blogger Post or Page:

https://www.youtube.com/watch?v=eHxhDzbGnaQ&spfreload=10

is the Blogger equivalent of the similar video created for Word-Press users.

Lastly in this section about pictures, I created a video on the use of a WordPress plugin called Tiled Galleries:

https://www.youtube.com/watch?v=IHWXh3kKeho

Honestly, it seems like there are a million plugins available to manipulate pictures; some are easy to use, some are less intuitive. Some are so feature-rich, it seems like they can do everything with regards to picture handling. I've used quite a few, but if I'm looking for just the creation of simple photo displays that look attractive as part of a post or page, I frequently turn to Tiled Galleries. This plugin is part of the Jetpack set of plugins and as such, is installed on many WordPress blogs. Have a look at this video and see if this plugin is something you could use.

Regardless of your skill level with pictures, you will inevitably run into the odd problem. I find that people often get in trouble with pictures when they fuss and fuss with them. I feel that if something goes wrong with the insertion of a picture, completely delete it from the post and start fresh.

Good luck with pictures!

Embedding Videos in WordPress or Blogger Posts or Pages

Another sticky subject is embedding videos – usually YouTube videos in either a WordPress or Blogger post or page. I've created two videos to walk you through the process:

How to Embed a YouTube video in a WordPress Post:
https://www.youtube.com/watch?v=Fhjoy6MzMvE

How to Insert a YouTube Video in a Blogger Post or Page:
https://www.youtube.com/watch?v=zXp-lI5B628

Although many see this as a difficult activity, you'll see from the videos that it's quite easy when you understand the basics.

Creating a Signature for the End of Your Post

As a teacher of WordPress, I always find it interesting to listen to some of the questions that crop up.

Several years ago, I was teaching a brand new and very technology-challenged author how to blog on WordPress. Her question to me was, "How do I tell where the end of one blog post is and the beginning of the next one is?"

Interesting question! I'd never questioned where the beginning and end of the posts were—I think my eyes had grown accustomed to finding them in whatever form they took. Let's face it, all blog setups are different and it can take some time to get used to the different arrangements.

Regardless of your skill level, your readers will have a variety of backgrounds. For that reason, as well as others, it's a good idea to create a signature, or sign-off for each blog post. This video:

https://www.youtube.com/watch?v=MAheCmM887s

provides a variety of examples for you to work your way through.

As I cover in the video, a signature can thank your readers for visiting, give your readers directions — to subscribe to your blog, perhaps — and make them aware of news. Regardless of how you put a signature in place and what it contains, it helps the technology-challenged readers to find the end of your blog post!

Creating Social Media Buttons in Code for Your Sidebar

Whether you have a Blogger blog or a WordPress blog, sometimes it's just nicer to create a unique selection of Social Media icons for your sidebar — different than what's available in some of the plugins, for example.

I mentioned previously in the discussion about organizing sidebars so that all of your social media buttons are near or at the top of your sidebar and, if possible, be together in one widget. This is a bit difficult to do on Blogger unless you know HTML code. And on WordPress, Goodreads and Amazon icons aren't included in most of the social media widgets.

I'm sure you're saying to yourself, "But I don't code." I don't really either. I do the cheater's method of coding. As I explain in the video here:

https://www.youtube.com/watch?v=dxqDti89gco

I create the arrangement of images or icons I want on a draft page and then copy the HTML code and paste it into a text widget on the sidebar.

Can I read code? Yes. I can also create it with a bit of thought, but more often than not I can't be bothered to do so when I know my blog will create it for me. To share how I do this, I created a video called The Cheater's Way of creating HTML Using a Blog Post or Page:

https://www.youtube.com/watch?v=c6jWVV9BWYQ

Although the example uses a WordPress blog, this method can be used for a Blogger blog also.

Placing HTML or iFrame Code on a Sidebar

We need to talk about putting other types of code on your sidebar and making it fit properly. One of my pet peeves is visiting blogs and seeing widgets overtake the sidebar, and in some cases, so big that half of it is off my screen!

As book bloggers, we often have the opportunity to put code on our sidebar. We can put code from Goodreads to show our latest reviews or show off our TBR shelf, or we can have a countdown clock to a much-anticipated release.

Including our example above, there are many reasons to put either HTML or iFrame code on our sidebars. Creating code that's properly sized is much easier than you think. Have a look at the video here:

https://www.youtube.com/watch?v=dxqDti89gco

for the WordPress example and here:

https://www.youtube.com/watch?v=jwtO-6-YXHM

for the Blogger example, and see for yourself how straightforward this can be!

Placing Pictures or Other Graphics on the Sidebar of your Blog

Like putting code on the sidebar of your blog and making it fit, putting a picture in place and making it fit is also a sticky problem for many bloggers.

You don't have a lot of choices for this activity on Blogger. This video walks you through the process:

https://www.youtube.com/watch?v=7Ywjvg08wTM

For those of you feeling a bit more adventuresome after all the videos you've watched, you can also put a picture on a draft page—size it properly—and then copy the HTML code and paste that into a text gadget on your sidebar. Pretty fancy!

For WordPress users, there are quite a few image widgets available for your use. There's the one that comes with Jetpack, but another of my favorites is Image Widget. Have a look at this video:

https://www.youtube.com/watch?v=yg7QAF6j1t0

Hotlinking pictures on the sidebars of both Blogger and WordPress

Attaching a URL to a picture is called "Hotlinking" and is a common activity for bloggers. What this does is attach a link to the picture allowing the reader to follow a link when they click on the picture. An example of this would be putting a book cover on the sidebar of your blog that is linked to the buy page on Amazon. Here are videos explaining how to do this on Blogger:

https://www.youtube.com/watch?v=eHxhDzbGnaQ&spfreload=10

and on WordPress:

https://www.youtube.com/watch?v=581QZAlMrFU

Sources of Pictures for Blog Posts

There are a number of websites where you can download graphic and photo images to use on your blog. Some are free and others come with a nominal price tag. Either way, it's advisable that you use these sites rather than simply taking an image off of a Google search as that image may be copyrighted to another source.

Free:

http://unsplash.com

http://pixabay.com

http://morguefile.com

http://photopin.com

http://gratisography.com

Paid:

http://istockphoto.com

http://bigstockphoto.com

http://dreamstime.com

http://123rf.com

http://shutterstock.com

YOUR HELPFUL HINTS ARE WAITING...

Interested in getting some FREE BOOKS filled with helpful hints and some helpful videos to your inbox. Hints that are directly applicable to what you do? Click here (http://bakerviewconsulting.com/helpful-hints-waiting/) to get started!

Glossary

Badge – A badge is a graphic that's used to advertise a blog or website. Typically, it's small and square (250px X 250px) and reflects the branding of the website.

Blog – A blog is a type of website, which allows information to be added in a static fashion as well as a serial fashion. It can be run on a wide variety of platforms or programs.

Blog Feed/Feed – The Blog Feed, typically shortened to "Feed," is also known as RSS or RSS feed. A Blog feed or a RSS feed is a standard Internet technology that allows updates of your blog to be delivered to various places – other websites like Goodreads or into feed-dreaders like Feedly. In terms of format, it's typically your blog's URL followed by a slash and then the word 'feed' or http://yourdomain.com/feed. It is possible that your blog's feed is different.

Blog Hop – A Blog Hop is an activity or game that's played using blogs with posts of a common theme. Everyone joining or playing the blog hop creates a post on their blog and then a clickable list is created of all the blogs participating with direct links to each post. This allows participants to easily click on links or hyperlinks and visit the blog posts of all the participants. Often the linking of the blogs is done using a free service called Linky (There are also paid versions of this type of service.). Linky will provide a form for entering each blogs' details and create code that can be placed on blogs allowing the list to be searchable and automatically updated as others join.

Blogging Platform – A Blogging Platform is the program used to operate or run a blog. There are several – the most popular being WordPress, Blogger, and Tumblr.

Blog reader/Feed reader – A blog reader or feed reader is a program that gathers the RSS feeds from blogs and display them to be read. Typically, this program provides a pleasing reading format and a method of keeping track of what's been read as well as what hasn't.

Book Blogger – a person who has a blog whose main focus is books.

Branding – Branding is the combination of the look, feel, and tone that creates a unified and identifiable collection of information.

Domain – also known as a URL – is the address of a website. It's typically in the format of http://yourdomainname.com

DRM encryption – DRM stands for Digital Rights Management. It's the type of encryption added to eBooks to control the use, modification, and distribution of copyrighted material. It can also be used for software and music.

Footer – The footer is the space at the very bottom of your website or blog. In some cases it can hold information in addition to a copyright statement.

Go Viral – this is a colloquial term to indicate massive dispersal. When talking about a blog post or a Facebook post, it's referred to as "Going Viral" when it attracts a lot of attention in the form of hits, shares, likes or whatever is appropriate to that particular platform.

Gravatar – a graphic that represents something – often a person. As an example, a gravatar is often seen beside any comment that a person makes on a blog post, Facebook or Twitter post.

Header – the Header is the part of a website at the top of the site and generally runs from side to side. It can also be used to refer to the top of a post – the area where the title is seen.

Hosting company – A Host or Hosting company is a business that has a collection of servers or big computers and sells space on those servers for people to run a blog or website. Examples would be Site Ground, GoDaddy or InMotion.

Hotlink – Hotlink is a common term to refer to a link that's attached to an image or some text in a website or blog. If a person clicks on that picture or text they are taken to another website. As an example, if a cover graphic of a book is 'hotlinked' to an Amazon buy link or URL, when it's clicked on, the direct buy page for that book on

Amazon is opened.

Keyword(s) – A Keyword is an important word or collection of words used to describe something. Keywords for a book would be words like the genre, the city the book is centered in, or the time period. Keywords for an author often refer to works they use to describe themselves, their work and content for their platform communications.

Linky List – or Linky is the common term that refers to a software program or website that allows for the gathering of information of like-themed blog posts and the display of these links on all blogs involved.

Meme – a game or group activity played on blogs and/or social media. There's a common theme, a loose collection of rules and an identifying feature. For example, there's a blog meme called Follow Friday that bloggers can play. They create a blog post, post the unifying graphic and often comment on the weekly theme. They add their URL and other details into a Linky List and then go visiting other participants. Likewise, a Twitter meme called #MondayBlogs has bloggers post a tweet with an eye-catching title, a direct URL and the hashtag MondayBlogs to their Twitter stream. They then retweet and visit and read the tweets/posts of other participants.

Menu Bar – a Menu Bar is typically a line of clickable links either just under the header of a website/blog or in the header area of a website. The clickable links lead to other parts of the website or blog.

Plugin – a piece of code added to a blog to perform a function on that blog. An example of a Plugin is Akismet – it helps segregate spam into a specific folder. Sometimes a Plugin can also function as a Widget. In that case, it will have a function on the sidebar of a blog or website. An example of that would be an Image Widget.

Post or blog post – A collection of words and pictures that are published and then visible on that blog. The word "Post" is frequently used to refer to an entry (often words and pictures) put on Facebook, Twitter, or other social media.

Re-Blog – to Re-blog is to copy and paste material from one blog post to another. It's either officially done by the 'Reblog' function available on several blogging platforms, or simply copy/paste. To avoid copyright issues, ensure proper attribution.

Search engine – A Search Engine is a very complicated computer program that searches a collection of websites to find entries for given words. An example is Google.

SEO – SEO stands for Search Engine Optimization. SEO is a collection of activities we perform on blogs/websites that make it easier for search engines to find and search them. These activities range from careful use of keywords, to linking to other blogs, to the addition of helpful information to pictures, among other examples.

Sidebar – The area on one or both sides of a website or blog. It contains content that's placed there often in the form of widgets or gadgets.

Tags – The word "Tag" or "Tags" has many meanings. Most commonly it refers to bits of HTML coding with specific meaning. The H1 tag stands for Heading 1 tag – meaning the highest level of heading. An "em" tag stands for italics and a "strong" tag stands for bold. Tags are said to be 'wrapped' around text. Tags have their own language of a sort where <h1> means start the h1 and </h1> means stop the h1. So, to wrap the text – <h1>The Title is Here</h1> will mark the phrase "The Title is Here" as the main title of a blog post. Similarly, Here will make the word "Here" appear bold.

Theme – A collection of coding that controls the look and feel of a blog.

URL – The direct link or hyperlink to a post. It can be referred to as a Domain, but can also be used to show the exact link to a specific entry on a website.

Website – A site on the Internet

Widget – A collection of code used to perform a specific function (usually) on the sidebar of a website or blog. An example of a widget is an Image Widget that is used to hold a picture on the sidebar of a WordPress blog.

About The Author

Social Media and Wordpress Consultant Barb Drozdowich has taught in colleges, universities and in the banking industry. More recently, she brings her 15+ years of teaching experience and a deep love of books to help authors develop the social media platform needed to succeed in today's fast evolving publishing world. She delights in taking technical subjects and making them understandable by the average person. She owns Bakerview Consulting and manages the popular blog, Sugarbeat's Books, where she talks about Romance novels.

She is the author of 9 books, over 30 YouTube videos and an online WordPress course, all focused on helping authors and bloggers. Barb lives in the mountains of British Columbia with her family.

Barb can be found:
Author Website: http://barbdrozdowich.com
Business Blog: http://bakerviewconsulting.com
Facebook Author Page: http://bit.ly/1XYKxyQ
Twitter: http://bit.ly/1U5PxMr
Google+: http://bit.ly/1XYKzGQ
Pinterest: http://bit.ly/1skDog8
Goodreads: http://bit.ly/1qVii6L
YouTube Channel: http://bit.ly/25uvqCQ
Tech Hints Newsletter: http://eepurl.com/DfCRj
Amazon Author Page: http://amzn.to/1TGSAuL
Newsletter link - http://bit.ly/1UmP231

Also by Barb Drozdowich

Top Advice for Authors Promoting Their Book: From a survey of 500+ book bloggers

As the old saying goes: "Get the truth right from the horse's mouth." In a recent survey of over 500 book bloggers and other bloggers who feature books, the question was asked: "If you could give an author one piece of advice about promoting their book, what would it be?" As you can well imagine if you asked 500+ people the same question, you would get a variety of responses, but you would also see repeats of areas of importance or of commonality. Get some ideas from the people who live to talk about books.

Top Advice for Authors Promoting Their Book is only available in e-format from your favorite retailer.

* * *

The Author's Platform: The Beginner's Guide

This book is aimed at authors who are new to the online aspect of book promotion and marketing. *The Author's Platform* clearly and simply explains all the various parts of an author's platform; what they are and what to do with them. This book uses simple, straightforward language. It helps beginner authors take a confident step into a world that is unfamiliar to them.

The Author's Platform is available at your favorite online retailer and the paperback copy can be ordered from your favorite bookstore.

* * *

Book Blog Tours: An Essential Marketing Tool for Authors

The world of *Book Blog Tours* is another world that many authors are unfamiliar with prior to publishing a book. This world has it's own language and norms. And this world is surrounded by mis-information and mis-understandings. *Book Blog Tours* is meant to demystify this world - serve as a primer to authors about to enter this world. *Book Blog Tours* explains all aspects of blog tours carried out by a company and provides enough guidance to an author interested in creating their own tour.

Book Blog Tours is available at your favorite online retailer and the paperback copy can be ordered from your favorite bookstore.

* * *

Keep your eyes peeled for a box set or two coming your way shortly as well as some new subjects to help authors and bloggers understand the technology that they need to work with.

69304956R00080

Made in the USA
Columbia, SC
18 April 2017